CROSS CULTURAL STUDIES ON THE FAMILY

CROSS CULTURAL STUDIES ON THE FAMILY

Edited By
SUNIL KUKREJA

SERIALS PUBLICATIONS
NEW DELHI

First Published - 2006

ISBN : 81-8387-024-4

Published by

SERIALS PUBLICATIONS
4830/24, Ansari Road, Darya Ganj
New Delhi-110002 (India)
Phone : 91-11-23245225
Fax : 91-11-23272135
E-mail: serials@satyam.net.in,
serialspublications@vsnl.net
Website : www.seriealspub.com

To my brothers and sisters

CONTENTS

PREFACE

In 2004 some basic changes in the *International Journal of Sociology of the Family* (*IJSF*) marked a tangible turning point for the publication. With a totally new editorial advisory board, a new publisher, and even a new look for the journal, my role as the new editor-in-chief of the journal was in earnest underway. Since its inception, the journal has been a mainstay in profiling scholarship and research on the sociology of the family, and this restructuring of the journal represents a renewed commitment to this tradition. I am grateful to Julia Adams, Paul Amato, Sara Arber, Scott Coltrane, Barbara Risman, Monserrat Sagot, and Pepper Schwartz for willing to be on the editorial advisory board.

Cross Cultural Studies on the Family, featuring a select number of pieces that appeared in Volume 31 (nos. 1 and 2) of *IJSF*, represents the joint commitment of International Journals Inc. and Serials Publications to more broadly profile some of the research and articles featured in *IJSF*.

This volume consists of nine chapters; each wholly self-contained and, as in another edited volume we completed recently featuring articles from our sister publication–*International Review of Modern Sociology*–the pieces here embody a strong flavor of interdisciplinary research. We are indeed very delighted to be affirming this tradition through the articles featured in the ensuing pages of this volume.

Chapters one and two analyze risky sexual behaviors among adolescents in the United States. In Chapter One, Debarun Majumdar and Roque Mendez primarily analyze the role of parental control, affect, and parental sexual permissiveness on adolescents' risky sexual behaviors measured through three different dimensions. While their findings confirm what might be a reasonable perception, that parental sexual permissiveness is associated with risky adolescent sexual behavior, they also affirm that adolescents with more controlling parents are prone to risky sexual behaviors. Majumdar and Roque's work here particularly reveals the differential impact of the father and mother, and helps to further clarify the way in which parental dynamics can potentially influence adolescents' sexuality. They report that excessive parental control, parental permissiveness, and a lack of family intimacy in the family are linked to risky adolescent sexual behaviors.

In Chapter Two, Debarun Majumdar emphasizes the differences in risky sexual practices along racial/ethnic lines. The study concentrates on data on Asian-American, Black, Hispanic, and White adolescents, and is consistent with other prior findings, which affirm the relatively higher sexual risk that Black adolescents confront; they have the highest rate of sexually transmitted diseases and were most likely to be sexually active before being 14 years of age. However, the study goes on to also point out that Asian-American adolescents–more than their counterparts from other ethic groups –are most prone to not using contraception while being sexually active. Majumdar further reflects on the salience of individual, cultural, and familial factors in interpreting the differences in outcomes for the four ethic groups.

In Chapter Three, Xiaowei Zang presents an analysis of love marriage in Malaysia. Centered along the differing trends among the Malays and Chinese, the analysis suggests that while the Chinese report higher levels of marriage based on love, the distinction between Chinese men and Malay men is less marked when controlling for background factors. In turn, the trend for Malay women is not quite in line with their male counterparts; leading the author to suggest ways in which gender appears to mediate the manner in which some critical cultural considerations shape the differential experience for Malay women.

Sue Ya Xu's discussion in Chapter Four examines one of the perennial concerns of working parents: child care for their young dependents. Xu's analysis looks at this issue by comparing some data on this issue among female state employees in China between 1970s-1990s. As China has undergone various facets of its economic reforms in the past decades, Xu's findings show that working mothers are also confronting new challenges in the getting child care; as state sponsored care has become increasingly limited, parents rely on help from family members or–for those who can afford it– commercially based childcare services. It would not be unreasonable if one were to view this trend in family-work life as another symptom of an increasingly stratified modern China.

In Chapter Five, Xiaolin Xie and Yan Xia examine generational differences in attitudes toward the elderly in China. Using data collected from Guangzhou in 2000, the authors find that "baby boomers" in general are more inclined than their younger counterparts to positively view the elderly. Interestingly, they report that male respondents were also more likely to report positive attitudes toward the elderly than female respondents. While the previous chapter by Xu highlights the impending concern about childcare for working parents in China, Xie and Xia's findings also raise some considerations about care–in this case, for the elderly– that will no doubt be widespread concern in China. How will changing attitudes about the elderly play into societal commitments about caring for them? The implications raised by Xie and Xia's focus clearly need to be considered.

Rosario Esteinou's examination of the growth of the nuclear family trend in Mexico provides a critical contrast to trends in the nuclear family pattern in western societies. Through a discussion of kinship relations, the nature of the family structure and family relationships during the colonial era in Mexico, Esteinou argues that contrary to conventional wisdom, the essential nature of nuclear family relations and structure in Mexico did not exactly take hold until the post-colonial era, while various traditional features of family structure remain within contemporary Mexican society.

In Chapter Seven, Akbar Aghajanian and Amir Mehryar trace the evolution of family planning policies in Iran beginning with some of the early initiatives in the 1920s. Their presentation especially puts into focus the significance of the state in attempting to control family size and the population growth rate. Further, their discussion sheds some light into some socio-economic motivations at the personal and family unit level that may be associated with trends in the family size in Iran.

Jeanne Stolzer focuses on breastfeeding in the penultimate chapter. Grounded in bioecological theory, Stolzer situates the systemic level considerations that inform biological, cultural, and social influences on breastfeeding. By reaffirming the salience of bioecological factors, this approach then affirms the relevance of considering a more comprehensive approach to framing the discourse on the practice of breastfeeding.

The last chapter focuses on issues of identity among Canadian youth of Bangladeshi descent. Highlighting the increasing relevance of Islam in their everyday life, Roksana Nazneen brings to fore the dynamic between first and second generation Muslim-Bangladeshi Canadians, and a discussion of why Islam–rather than grounding in Canadian or Bangladeshi culture is gaining deeper acceptance among these youth.

Finally, on a personal note, I am deeply grateful to my bothers, sisters, and family who have been a tremendous source of energy, support and inspiration for me through the years. Circumstances may have been such that though we have not been together as much over the past couple of decades, yet they've never ever been far from my thoughts. I am also most thankful to my dear wife Laura who has been a bottomless well of support. I am truly fortunate indeed.

Sunil Kukreja
Tacoma, Washington

CONTRIBUTORS

Debarun Majumdar, Ph.D., is an Assistant Professor of sociology at Texas State University. His research interests are in demography, quantitative methodology, and adolescent health. His recent publications include: "Choosing Childlessness: Intentions of Voluntary Childlessness in the United States" in *Michigan Sociological Review,* 2004, 18: 108-135. Along with Wendy Manning, Pamela Smock, he is co-author of "The Relative Stability of Cohabiting and Marital Unions for Children", in *Population Research and Policy Review,* 2004, 23 (4): 135-159.

Roque V. Mendez, Ph.D. is professor of psychology at Texas State University. His interests are in HIV/AIDS prevention and cultural issues. A recent publication of his in *Current Psychology* (Winter, 2002) is entitled: "Multiple Partners in the Age of AIDS: Self-consciousness Theory and HIV Risk Behavior."

Xiaowei Zang teaches sociology at the City University of Hong Kong and is the author of *Children of the Cultural Revolution* (Westview Press, 2000), *Elite Dualism and Leadership Selection in China* (RoutledgeCurzon, 2004), and many refereed articles in journals in the U.S., including those in *The Sociological Quarterly*, *Sociological Perspectives*, *Sociological Focus*, *International Sociology*, and *Social Science Research*.

Sue Y. Xu works at the Children, Schools, and Families division of Hertfordshire County Council in the UK. Prior to this, she was a research fellow at the Faculty of Social Sciences, Erasmus University of Rotterdam, and has also been a research fellow at the Institute of Economic Research in Development and Reform Committee (China). Her main research interests include population dynamics, women and the labor market, and school-employment transitions. She is currently working on a project studying the life-experiences of young people who have been excluded from schools.

Xiaolin Xie, is an Associate Professor in Family and Child Studies in the School of Family, Consumer and Nutrition Sciences in Northern Illinois University at DeKalb, IL. She can be contacted at *xiaolinx@niu.edu.*

Dr. Yan Xia is an Assistant Professor in Family and Consumer Sciences in the University of Nebraska-Lincoln. She can be contacted at *yxia@mail.unomaha.edu.*

Rosario Esteinou is a professor and a researcher at the Research and Higher Studies in Social Anthropology Center in Mexico city. As a sociologist of the family, she has analyzed some of the characteristics of mexican families particularly, but not exclusively, in the middle classes. Some of the areas she has focused on are: survival strategies, level and quality of life, family values, role structure, couple formation patterns and parenting. More recently, concerned with searching a wider conceptual framework, she has considered the anthropological, demographical and historical perspectives to understand the evolution of family forms in Mexican society.

Akbar Aghajanian is Professor of Sociology at Fayetteville State University. He received his PhD from Duke University. His research training is in demography and he has published widely in the area of family and demography in Iran. He has received grants from National Science Foundation, Department of Education, and a number of private foundations to support his research and training activities. He is currently the Director of Research Center for Health Disparities at Fayetteville State University.

Amir H. Mehryar is Professor of Behavioral Science at the Institute for Research in Planning and Development. He received his PhD from University of London and has completed postdoctoral research at Harvard University and University of Pennsylvania. He has been resident research scientist at World Health Organization. Dr. Mehryar is currently the director of Regional Center for Population Studies and Research in Asia and the Pacific, Tehran, Iran.

Dr. Stolzer is currently an Assistant Professor in the Family Studies program at the University of Nebraska-Kearney. She is an advisory board member for the International Center for the Study of Psychiatry and Psychology (ICSPP). Dr. Stolzer teaches infant, child and adolescent, and lifespan development classes and is also an active researcher. Her research interests include cross-cultural parenting styles, the biocultural implications of breastfeeding, and attachment parenting.

Roksana Nazneen is Assistant Professor in the Sociology and Anthropology Department, Concordia University in Montreal. A Bangladeshi-Canadian, Nazneen received her doctoral degree in 2000. Her research areas are race and ethnicity, Bangladeshi/ Muslim women, multiculturalism and immigration. Nazneen is also an accomplished novelist in Bangladesh.

THE INFLUENCE OF PARENTAL AFFECT, CONTROL, AND SEXUAL PERMISSIVENESS ON RISKY SEXUAL BEHAVIORS AMONG SEXUALLY ACTIVE ADOLESCENTS IN THE UNITED STATES

1

Debarun Majumdar and Roque Mendez

INTRODUCTION

About three out of four adolescents have experienced sexual intercourse by their late teen years in the United States (CDC, 2000). It is no surprise then, that STDs and unwanted pregnancy rates remain high among adolescents. For example, young people ages 15 to 24 accounted for 48 percent of all STD cases in 2000 even though they comprised only 25 percent of the sexually experienced population (Weinstock, 2004). While these statistics are staggering, many public health experts fear that STDs may be more prevalent in this age group than these reports indicate. Young people, especially males, are less likely to seek medical care because they lack insurance or fear loss of confidentiality (Elliot, 2004). Moreover, many infections—including chlamydia, genital herpes, trichomoniasis and human papillomavirus—are asymptomatic (Weinstock, 2004). Young people may not obtain medical care or report infections until complications occur.

While STDs remain high among adolescents, unwanted pregnancies have declined. Teenage pregnancies fell by 28 percent nationwide since 1990 (Guttmacher Institute report, 2004). The inconsistencies between high rates of STDs and declining pregnancies may be due to the effectiveness of some contraceptive methods to prevent pregnancy, but not protect against infections (Center for Health and Healthcare in the Schools, 2004; Kaplan, 2001). Still, pregnancies among adolescents remain a concern. Of 900,000 pregnancies among adolescents, one third occur in women ages 17 or younger (Kaplan, 2001).

Condom use remains the one of the best ways to decrease the rates of unintended pregnancies and STDs, and educating youth in school settings on sexual risks and the proper use of condoms has been one of the most common and most effective means of increasing condom use (Kaplan, 2001). But, this may not be enough. Involving parents has been the key goal of several educational programs (Cates, 2004; Kaplan, 2001). The family is considered a critical influence in the sexual behavior of adolescents (Miller, 2002; Resnick, 1997). And including parents in intervention programs may not have come at a better time. Young people report that they are not able to discuss intimate sexual topics with their parents or fear reprisals from parents for disclosing information (Cates, 2004; Center for Health and Healthcare in the Schools, 2004). Our aim in this article is to examine the influence of parental involvement on adolescent condom use, pregnancy and STD rates. We hope to provide a better understanding of how these sexual risks are tempered or increased by parental or familial involvement. Such an understanding may prove useful in developing educational programs that target adolescents and their parents.

LITERATURE REVIEW

Emery (1992) suggests that intimacy and power are the basic dimensions around which relationships between parents and children evolve. Intimacy is expressed as affection and nurturance toward others and power as control, dominance or social influence over others. The constructs of intimacy and power have been supported by factor analytic work (Kiesler, 1983) and have been regarded by those in developmental research as the two key parenting styles that are basic to the healthy social and emotional development of children (Baumrind, 1971; Maccoby and Martin, 1983). Schaefer (1959) in his seminal work on parenting styles called these dimensions affect and control.

Intimacy or affect relates to the emotional relationship between parents and their children. Intimacy is based on the parent's and the child's perceptions of or desires for closeness with each other (Emery, 1992). Symbols of closeness (i.e. expressed emotions or affect) define the level of intimacy in a parent-child dyad (Emery, 1992). The lack of closeness marks indifference and consequently, the lack of parental expressed affect toward a child. Perceived warmth and caring expressed between parents and children, often measured as a process variable of parental support (Field, 1995; Markham, et.al. 2003), has been linked to less risk taking in adolescents. For example, adolescents whose parents expressed greater affect for them were less sexually experienced (Perkins and Luster, 1998). And, adolescents with parents they perceived to be supportive and caring were also more likely to be monogamous or use condoms (Luster and Small, 1994). Moreover, the more adolescents liked their mothers, the less likely they were to initiate sexual activity or become pregnant (Dittus and Jacard, 2000). Finally, female teens who were emotionally close to parents had a reduced risk of ever being pregnant or ever having had sex (Markham et al., 2003).

Power, by contrast, relates to dominance, control and influence in a dyad. Power or control as we will also refer to this construct, is continually being tested between parents and children who either do not exercise self-regulation or who desire greater autonomy (i.e. to make independent decisions) as they age (Emery, 1992). A delicate balance between parental control and adolescent independence is achieved in the developmental phases as children demand greater autonomy and parents relinquish control.

There are parents, however, who exert little or no control over their children's lives, and parents who maintain or exert greater control as children age. Parental permissiveness and authoritarian control have been conceptualized as extremes (Schaefer, 1959) and have been linked to risk behaviors. The research that we review, however, treats these parenting styles as independent constructs. For example, an adolescent's perception of how lenient and accepting parents are of sexual behaviors increases their levels sexual risk-taking behaviors (Jaccard and Dittus, 2000; Miller, Forehand, and Kotchick, 1999). Adolescents may perceive parental sexual permissiveness to be a sign of approval to engage in sexual activities themselves. Not having learned values that serve them at self-regulation and without clear guidelines, adolescents act impulsively and irresponsibly (Maccoby and Martin, 1982). Similarly, daughters who perceive their parents as having too many rules and controlling their behavior were more likely to be sexually active than those daughters whose parents have fewer rules, while boys with controlling parents were more likely to have initiated sex at an earlier age than those boys whose parents were not as controlling (Upchurch, 1999). Moreover, daughters whose parents have used psychological control (i.e. guilt) were less likely to have used condoms consistently and to have had more sexual partners (Rodgers, 1999). Often, parental control implies mistrust of the child and is likely to foster children who are aggressive and low in self-worth (Maccoby and Martin, 1982). Engaging in high-risk behaviors in such restrictive environments may simply be a form of rebelliousness, an adolescent's attempts at asserting their independence (Brehm and Brehm, 1981).

Parenting, however, involves both the use of power and intimacy (Emery, 1992). Both may be intricately intertwined (Emery, 1992). Parental supervision or monitoring of adolescents, for example, has been linked to fewer conduct problems and behavioral risks in adolescents (Frick, 1993; Rodgers, 1999), and more specifically to later sexual debut, monogamy and condom use (Donneberg, 2002; Luster and Small, 1994; Perkins and Luster, 1998; Resnick, 1997; Wilder and Watt, 2002). Parental supervision may exemplify both parental intimacy and control. Parents manage a balance of caring and sensitive parenting with appropriate discipline and intrusiveness. A balance of intimacy and control are considered ideal parenting styles (Maccoby and Martin, 1983) and may moderate high-risk behaviors in adolescents.

Studies show, however, that adolescent girls and boys may be affected differently by parental variables. Parental support, for example, was more likely to benefit daughters than sons; daughters with supportive parents were less sexually experienced (Markham et al., 2003; Small and Luster, 1994b). These gender differences may be due to ways in which parents respond differently to their sons and daughters. Sons receive more directives, greater pressure and fewer explanations than daughters, while daughters are more comforted by their parents than sons (Morrongiello and Dawber, 1999). Moreover, girls are increasingly less likely than boys to be given greater freedoms as they age (Bulcroft, Carmody and Bulcroft, 1996). Given these differences we believe that disaggregating the data by gender may give us a greater understanding of what parental factors influences male and female adolescents. Furthermore, the focus of past studies has been predominantly on parental influences.

In this study, we attempt to differentiate between the mother's and father's influence on adolescent sexual activity where possible.

HYPOTHESES

We believe intimacy and control to be key dimensions in family relationships. Intimacy as expressed affect decreases sexual activity among adolescents by forming strong influential social bonds that protects adolescents from harm (Markham et al., 2003; Metzler et al, 1994; Romer et al., 1994; Small and Luster, 1994a). Lower levels of parental permissiveness of sexual activity decreases risky behavior among adolescents by reinforcing beliefs and values that keep them from undesired outcomes (Jaccard and Dittus, 2000; Miller et al., 1999). With clearer guidelines and self-regulation, adolescents are more likely to act responsibly. And less restrictive parents have less rebellious and risk taking adolescents (Rodgers, 1999; Upchurch, 1999). In general, past studies on adolescent sexual behavior show that family processes such as support, lack of excess control, and disapproval of sexual activity reduces likelihood of risk-taking among teenagers. We expect these parental factors will reduce adolescent sexual risk by strengthening familial and social ties that keep adolescents away from unconventional behaviors.

Family process variables such as parental affect, sexual permissiveness, and control have been examined in a piecemeal fashion in past research. We consider these dimensions to be parts to a whole, and thus, this study takes a more comprehensive approach than previous studies. Their inclusion together may provide a better understanding of how the family impacts the chances of risky sexual behavior among adolescents. In particular, the influence of *parental affect or intimacy* on adolescent sexual behavior has been largely ignored in past research as focus of past research has traditionally been on parental control, supervision, and permissiveness. By including this dimension to the conventional family process variables, the literature is being further extended.

METHODS

Data and Participants

We analyzed contractual data from the Wave I of the school-based National Longitudinal Study of Adolescent Health (Add

Health 1995, Udry, 2003). The dataset contains a broad array of information related to adolescents' family, peers, relationships, as well as sexual behavior and other topics. Clustered sampling technique was used to collect this nationally representative data of US schools by region, urbanicity, school size, school type and ethnicity. A complete version of the research design is also available (Harris, Florey, Tabor, Bearman et al., 2003). The data was collected in a 90-minute in-home interview of the adolescents. Sensitive questions were carefully recorded by having adolescents enter responses directly into a computer with the help of audio CASI (Computer-assisted self-interviewing). This reduced the chances of social desirability for responses and interviewer bias. The analytical sample consisted of 3,652 male and 3,856 female adolescents who were sexually experienced. This was the baseline sample before list-wise deletion. This sample was taken from a larger set consisting of 20,745 adolescents between seventh and twelfth grades from 80 high schools and 52 middle schools. The sample did not include adolescents younger than eleven years due to the possibility of childhood sexual abuse (Abma, Driscoll, and Moore, 1998; Hofferth, Kahn, and Baldwin, 1987).

Measures

Outcome variables. We identified three dichotomous outcome variables that indicate risky sexual behavior. These variables have been used as sexual risk outcomes for adolescents in past research (Dittus & Jaccard, 2000; Luster & Small, 1994; Markham, Tortolero, 2003; Miller, 1999). The first variable is ever getting pregnant. The analytical sample for this outcome is restricted to girls. The second variable is ever having had any STD, such as chlamydia, gonorrhea, syphilis, HIV/AIDS, genital herpes, genital warts, or trichomoniasis. The third variable is non-use of condoms during the most recent intercourse. These outcome variables are indicative of risky sexual behavior and have also been used in previous studies such as, Majumdar, 2005; Wilder and Watt, 2002; Markham et al., 2003.

Parental Factors as Predictors. We identified 31 family process items related to parental affection, expressiveness, emotions, control, and permissive attitudes from the ADD Health questionnaire. To reduce the number of items to a few parsimonious descriptors, we performed a factor analysis using a principal components methods with a varimax rotation on the selected items (See Appendix A for items and factor loadings). Only those factors with eigenvalues of 1.0 or above were accepted. Moreover, a decision was made, a priori, to define the factors on the basis of items with coefficients loading .40 or above. This technique of extracting and rotating items produces a few orthogonal and interpretable groupings of items and is a recommended first step when factor analyzing a data set for the first time (SPSS, 1998).

Four factors pertaining to family processes emerged from the results of the factor analysis. The factors were named based on the higher item loadings for each factor (see Appendix A). The items of the first factor were related to the emotional aspects of father-adolescent relationship such as adolescents' perception of their paternal warmth, love, and care. We named this factor *Father Affect.* The items in the second factor represent the adolescents' perception of their mothers' affection toward them. Affective emotions included love, care, intimacy, and support. This factor was named *Mother Affect.* Because the factor analysis separated father's and mother's affect, adolescents with single parents are not included in the analysis. This is a shortcoming of this research, yet, it is important to understand the impact fathers and mothers have on adolescents' sexual activity. This approach also adds to previous literature in that it captures the nuance between father's and mother's influence, which are usually combined in past studies. The items in the third scale reflect the adolescents' perception of how lenient and how approving their parents are on matters pertaining to sexual activity. We called this factor *Parental Sexual Permissiveness.* We called the fourth scale *Parental Control.* The items in this factor were dichotomous and measured whether or not parents allowed adolescents to make decisions in several areas of their lives such as friendships, attire, TV viewing habits, and curfew.

A composite summative score for each factor was constructed from the items loading on each factor. Some of the items were reversed. Higher composite scores indicate higher levels of Father Affect, Mother Affect, Parental Sexual Permissiveness and Parental Control, respectively. The items were standardized because the levels varied across the items.

We then performed reliability analysis on each set of items of each factor to assess their internal consistency. The internal consistency for Father Affect, Mother Affect and Parental Sexual Permissiveness was acceptable with alphas of 0.82, 0.87 and 0.89, respectively. Internal consistency for Parental Control was 0.68. The alpha for this dichotomous variable was expected to be low due to the narrowness of score range (Downie & Heath, 1965).

Covariates. In the multivariate analyses, we adjusted for age, household income, religiosity, family structure, race or ethnicity. These covariates are related to adolescent sexual activity and have been used in previous studies (McLanahan and Sandefur, 1994; Mosher and McNally, 1991; Wu and Martinson, 1993). The parents of adolescents reported household income. The log-version of income is used for analyses. About 25% of the cases had missing information on this variable and we used regression analysis to estimate the income for these cases. Using an OLS model, with parental education, race/ethnicity, and family structure as predictors we estimate the household income for the missing cases. Religiosity was measured from the question "How important is religion to you?" The responses range from very important (4) to not important at all (1). Adolescents who indicate having no religion are assigned to the "not important at all" category. Family structure is indicated by two-parent biological, two-parent step, and other types that include adoptive and foster families. Race or ethnicity is categorized as black, Hispanic, other, and white. The "other" category includes Native Americans, Asians, and Pacific Islanders. Dummy variables are included for the income and religiosity variables as data had to estimated or assigned.

Data Analysis

Due to the complex nature of the clustered sample, we used STATA/SE software for the statistical analysis. The adolescent weights were applied to account for the design effects using STATA. Because gender differences have been noted in studies that have examined the relationship between parental variables and adolescent sexual behavior, we performed separate analysis for males and females.

The first set of analyses consisted of a series of chi-square tests to examine gender differences in the dependent variables. In the second set of analyses, multiple logistic regression models were developed to examine the association between the four parental factors and the dichotomous outcome variables. Logistic regression was used due to the binary nature of the dependent variables. A specific sequence of entering the independent variables was followed. The parental variables were added in the first model (Model I). The covariates were added next to examine if the effects of the key independent variables were mitigated (Model II). Results from both models are presented below.

RESULTS

Sample Description

The sample description by percentages and means is presented in Table 1. Almost one in five sexually active adolescent girls

Table 1
Characteristics of Sexually Experienced Adolescents

Characteristic	*Males*[a] *n=3,856*	*Females*[a] *n=3,652*	*Sexually experienced n=7,508*
Dependent Variables[b]			
Ever pregnant[c]	-	19.2	9.0
Ever had STD	3.7**	11.2	7.3
No condom at last sex	38.6**	50.5	44.2
Independent Variables (means)			
Father affection[d]	-1.1	-1.8	-1.4
Mother affection[d]	0.8	-0.9	0.0
Parental control[d]	0.0	-0.4	-0.2
Parental sexual permissiveness[d]	1.4	-2.4	-0.3
Covariates			
Household income (in '000s, mean)	40.6	41.1	40.8
Religiosity (mean)	2.7	2.9	2.8
Age	16.9	16.9	16.9
Family Structure			
Two-parent bio	64.3	61.1	62.3
Two-parent step	17.5	17.0	17.3
Other	18.2	22.0	20.0
Race/ethnicity			
Non-Hispanic white	59.0	65.0	61.9
Non-Hispanic black	25.6	22.3	24.0
Hispanic	12.6	10.1	11.4
Other	2.8	2.6	2.7

Source: Add Health Wave 1 (1995)
** $p<0.01$
[a] Percentages and means are weighted
[b] Gender difference tests only for dependent variables
[c] Sample restricted to females
[d] Scales based on standardized items; higher values indicate higher levels of the variable

had experienced pregnancy. A significantly higher percentage of sexually active females ever had STD compared to males (11.2 percent vs. 3.7 percent). Additionally, a significantly higher percentage of sexually active adolescent females did not use condoms at their last sexual intercourse compared to their male counterparts (50.5 percent vs. 38.6 percent). Sexually active boys perceived higher levels of both paternal (-1.1 to -1.8) and maternal (0.8 to–0.9) affect than girls. Perception of parental control was higher among boys than girls (0.0 vs. –0.4). Girls' perception of parental sexual permissiveness was lower than boys (-2.4 vs. 1.4).

The mean age of sexually active male and female respondents was 16.9 years. For both boys and girls, majority of the adolescents were whites, followed by blacks, Latinos, and others. At least 60 percent of both male and female respondents lived with both biological parents and another17 percent of them belonged to two-parent step-families. The parents of boys and girls reported a mean household income of about $41,00. The adolescents expressed adequate levels of importance of religion in their lives with girls indicating slightly higher levels (2.9) than boys (2.7).

Multivariate Analyses

Results from the multiple logistic regression analyses are presented in Tables 2 through 4. In these analyses, models that predicted various risky sexual behaviors by parental factors were developed. Model 1a shows that increased levels of parental control and parental sexual permissiveness significantly increased the odds of ever being pregnant for girls (Table 2). Net of the socio-demographic covariates (Model IIa), the effects of parental control and permissiveness remained significant. Father's affection marginally reduced the chances of pregnancy among girls (p=0.077). Among the covariates, higher levels of religiosity were associated with lower odds of ever experiencing a pregnancy.

The prediction models for STDs among boys and girls are presented in Table 3. The odds of ever having contracted an STD were significantly lowered with increased levels of father's affect for girls (Model Ib). However, parental sexual permissiveness was positively associated with STDs. After adjusting for the socio-demographic covariates, the directions

Table 2
Multivariate Logistic Regression Predicting Adolescent Pregnancy by Parental Factors

	Ia Ever Pregnant[a]		*IIa* Ever Pregnant[a]	
	OR	*t*	*OR*	*t*
Independent Variables				
Father Affect	0.96	-1.57	0.95[#]	-1.79
Mother Affect	0.99	-0.68	0.98	-0.98
Parental Control	1.08**	2.99	1.06*	2.16
Permissiveness	1.07***	4.30	1.07***	4.80
Covariates				
Age			1.14	1.59
Income (log)			0.78	-1.72
Religiosity			1.43*	2.38
Family Structure				
Two-Parent step			0.79	-0.85
Other			1.22	0.70
Two-parent bio[b]			-	-
Race/Ethnicity				
Black			1.50	1.43
Hispanic			1.18	0.70
Other			1.24	0.43
White[b]			-	-
Missing Dummies				
Income			0.97	-0.12
Religiosity			0.72	0.11
F	7.53	5.43		
N	1,791	1,772		

Source: Add Health Wave 1 (1995)
[#]$p<0.10$ *$p<0.05$ **$p<0.01$ ***$p<0.0001$
[a] Sample restricted to females
[b] Reference categories

of father's affect and parental sexual permissiveness remained stable, although the impact of the former diminished slightly (p=0.056). Mother's affect and parental control were not significantly related to STD experience among girls. The odds of ever having an STD were significantly higher for black adolescents girls compared to whites. Additionally, adolescents' age was positively associated with their chances of ever having contracted an STD.

Table 3
Multivariate Logistic Regression Predicting Adolescents ever having had STDs by Parental Factors

	Female				*Male*			
	Model Ib		*Model IIb*		*Model Ic*		*Model IIc*	
	OR	*t*	*OR*	*t*	*OR*	*t*	*OR*	*t*
Father Affect	0.94*	-1.97	0.95#	-1.94	0.95	-0.54	0.94	-0.66
Mother Affect	1.00	0.12	0.99	-0.56	1.02	0.33	1.01	0.19
Parental Control	1.04	1.25	1.05	1.52	1.07*	2.14	1.07*	1.96
Permissiveness	1.07**	3.34	1.05*	2.52	1.11**	3.25	1.08*	2.28
Covariates								
Age			1.53**	3.38			1.31	1.80
Income (log)			1.11	0.66			0.87	-0.65
Religiosity			1.09	0.55			1.17	0.45
Family Structure								
Two-parent step			1.24	0.89			1.01	0.02
Other			1.15	0.39			1.97	1.38
Two-parent bio[a]			-	-			-	-
Race/Ethnicity								
Black			2.53**	3.24			2.80*	2.09
Hispanic			0.70	-0.72			2.22	1.62
Other			1.16	0.30			0.06**	-3.16
White[a]			-	-			-	-
Missing Dummies								
Income			0.97	-0.10			0.77	-0.50
Religiosity			2.05	1.50			1.63	0.54
F	3.46		4.02		3.66		4.27	
N	1,802		1,783		2,009		1,989	

Source: Add Health Wave 1 (1995).
#p<0.10 *p<0.05 **p<0.01 ***p<0.0001; [a] Reference categories

Among sexually experienced boys, increase in the levels of parental control and parental sexual permissiveness increased the odds of ever having had STDs in both the unadjusted and adjusted models (Model Ic, IIc). Neither mother's nor father's affect were related to STDs for boys. The chances of ever having an STD among boys were significantly higher among blacks and lower among adolescents of other races compared to whites.

Table 4 shows the odds of not using condoms during most recent sexual intercourse for boys and girls who are sexually active. The likelihood of girls' partners not using a condom was directly associated with sexual permissiveness of parents (Model Id). The inclusion of the covariates did not mitigate this effect (Model IId). Among the covariates, chances of not using condoms were higher among sexually active Hispanics girls and those of other races and ethnicities compared to whites. Increase in the levels of religiosity among girls was positively associated with the chances of not using condoms. Finally, those who had missing information on religiosity or those who indicated they had "no religion" were at increased risk of not using condoms at most recent sex.

Table 4
Multivariate Logistic Regression Predicting Adolescent Condom Nonuse by Parental Factors

	Female				*Male*			
	Model Ib		*Model IIb*		*Model Ic*		*Model IIc*	
	OR	*t*	*OR*	*t*	*OR*	*t*	*OR*	*t*
Father Affect	0.96	-1.92	0.96	-1.65	1.01	0.66	1.01	0.65
Mother Affect	1.02	1.94	1.01	1.64	0.97*	-2.49	0.97*	-2.12
Parental Control	1.01	0.53	1.01	0.31	1.03	1.47	1.04	1.90
Permissiveness	1.04**	3.43	1.04***	4.19	1.00	0.31	1.01	0.47
Covariates								
Age			1.03	0.37			1.11	1.72
Income (log)			0.98	-0.21			0.87	-1.59
Religiosity			1.31**	2.83			0.94	-0.82
Family Structure								
Two-parent step			0.98	-0.09			1.07	0.50
Other			0.87	-0.76			1.20	0.72
Two-parent bio[a]			-	-			-	-
Race/Ethnicity								
Black			0.75	-1.62			0.56**	-3.15
Hispanic			1.86**	2.90			0.76	-1.18
Other			2.38**	2.63			1.29	0.97
White[a]			-	-			-	-
Missing Dummies								
Income			1.06	0.47			1.01	0.05
Religiosity			2.72**	3.41			0.72	-1.61
F	3.88		3.37		2.28		2.17	
N	1,802		1,783		2,009		1,989	

Source: Add Health Wave 1 (1995).
*$p<0.05$ **$p<0.01$ ***$p<0.0001$; [a] Reference category

Of all the family processes, mother's affect significantly reduced the chances of not using condoms during last sexual intercourse for sexually experienced boys in both models Ie and IIe. Among the covariates, adolescents' race and ethnicity was related to the lack of condom use. Specifically, black teenagers were significantly less likely to not having used condoms during most recent sexual intercourse compared to whites.

DISCUSSION

The primary goal of this study was to examine parental influence on risky behavior among adolescents. We began by identifying parental variables from a list of family process variables available in the ADD Health 1995 survey by using factor analysis. Then a series of logistic regressions were performed to examine the effect of parental factors on adolescent sexual activity. From the results emerged a clearer picture of the influence of parents on adolescent sexual risk taking. There were three key findings and each of these is discussed at greater length below. One, permissive parental attitudes toward sex was a prominent factor across all of the outcome variables. The leniency of parents was associated with enhanced the chances of risky sexual behavior among sexually active youth. Two, relationships within the family have substantial bearing upon the sexual behavior and outcomes of adolescents. Fathers' and mothers' affect appeared to be linked with reduced sexual risk of boys and girls differently. Lastly, more parental control was linked to increased risk in adolescent sexual behavior.

Permissiveness, or the lack of control, was a prevalent factor. Adolescent girls whose parents are more permissive toward sex were more likely to not have used condoms and to have been pregnant. Boys with the similar parents were more likely to have had STDs. Prior studies have found this (Miller et al, 1999; Small and Luster, 1994a). In short, permissive parents have permissive adolescents. Those with permissive parents act on decisions that, unfortunately, have dire consequences. Conversely, adolescents whose parents disapprove of risky sexual behaviors take precautions that protect them from undesirable outcomes.

Fathers' and mothers' affect toward their children was also important in two respects. First, girls with more accepting and loving fathers had lowered chances of acquiring STDs ($p = 0.056$) and ever being pregnant ($p = 0.077$), while boys with more loving mothers had used condoms most recently. The risk effect of fathers on the girls is understandable. Most importantly, a sense of connectedness (i.e. closeness, warmth, caring) allows for greater ways by which a father may influence a daughter's healthy development (Markham, Tortolero, Escobar-Chaves,

Parcel, Harrist & Abby, 2003). A close relationship may provide an influential and protective barrier to high risk sexual behaviors. By contrast, young adolescent girls with indifferent or rejecting fathers seek substitutes or father figures by engaging in sex with multiple partners (Belsky, Steinberg, & Draper, 1991). Thus, girls whose fathers are more affective are less at risk to contract STDs and get pregnant.

The mother's affect on boys' recent use of condoms, on the other hand, is a bit more puzzling. We assume that mothers may also have a more protective influence over their son's development when their relationship is close (Markham, Tortolero, Escobar-Chaves, Parcel, Harrist and Abby, 2003). Mothers who are disinterested or detached from their sons may not have the same effect. These results, however, merit further research. Currently, there is not sufficient research on mother-specific or father-specific emotional relationships and risky sexual behavior among adolescents. Further investigation may give us a better understanding of the relationship between adolescents' perception of emotionality with their parents and their risky sexual behavior.

In line with some past research, this study showed that parental control was linked to an increased likelihood of engaging in risky sexual behaviors (Upchurch et al., 1999). Adolescent girls with more controlling parents were more likely to have been pregnant and adolescent boys with similar parents were more likely to have had STDs. Controlling parents may trigger rebelliousness and reactivity in adolescents who are coming of age as adults (Brehm and Brehm, 1981) or, alternatively, parents may be exercising greater control on their teenage children that have experienced undesired outcomes.

These three findings highlight the importance of the key dimensions of control and intimacy. Excessive control, the lack of control (i.e. permissiveness) and the lack of intimacy are parental conditions that do not allow for the healthy development of adolescents as they navigate through challenging years in which they explore their sexuality and come of age. The right amount of control and intimacy provides guidance, direction, encouragement and a certain influential protection against high-risk sexual behaviors.

Although the findings from this study enabled us to better understand the dynamics between family processes, the role of intimacy and control in the family processes and risky sexual behaviors among sexually active teenagers, there are several limitations to the study. Due to the cross-sectional nature of the data, no causal relationships can be inferred. It is possible that exhibiting higher sexual risk may lead to lower parental affect than the other way around. We could not separately examine the effects of monitoring and permissiveness of mothers and fathers due to unavailability of data. The internal consistency of the parental control variable is low. This can be improved by questions that have a greater spread of response categories, for example, using a Likert scale. Because we evaluated father's and mother's affect individually, single parent families were excluded from this analysis. Furthermore, we based our parental constructs on the results of the exploratory factor analysis. This approach kept us from differentiating between mother's and father's permissiveness. Future research might examine whether the effect of parental sexual permissiveness on risky behavior varies with the gender of the parents. We were also limited regarding the parental control variable because the variable's items were not distinguishable by the parent's gender. Finally, the mechanism underlying the reduction of sexual risks due to parental affect remains unknown. These limitations can be addressed in future research. Moreover, examining these relationships by race and ethnicity would further advance the understanding of adolescent sexual risks.

Stemming infection rates among the young may be a challenge. Approximately 14% high school students in a nationwide project, for example, reported having four or more partners (Cates, 2004). And infections like chlamydia and gonorrhea spread more easily and quickly among adolescent women and their partners (Cates, 2004). Nevertheless, parents can be key in influencing the lives of adolescents. The current study demonstrates how parents can lessen and as well as elevate the chances of sexual risks among adolescents, and recommendations that emphasize the inclusion of parents in helping reduce sexual risks among adolescents should be acted on (Department of Health and Human Services, 2001) to reduce the high costs of STDs and unwanted pregnancies to our families and society.

REFERENCES

Abma, J.C., Driscoll, A., and Moore, K. (1998), Young Women's Degree of Control Over First Intercourse: An Exploratory Analysis. *Family Planning Perspectives, 30*, 12-18.

Baumrind, D. (1971), Current Patterns of Parental Authority. *Developmental Psychology Monograph*, 4 (1, pt.2).

Belsky, J., Steinberg, L. & Draper, P. (1991), Childhood Experience, Interpersonal Development and Reproductive Strategy: An Evolutionary theory of Socialization. *Child Development, 62,* 647-670.

Brehm S.S. & Brehm, J.W. (1981), *Psychological Reactance: A theory of Freedom and control.* New York: Academic Press.

Bulcroft, R.A., Carmody, D.C., Bulcroft, K.A. (1996), Patterns of Parental Independence Giving to Adolescents: Variations by Race, Age, and Gender of Child. *Journal of Marriage and the Family, 58* (4), 866-883.

Cates, J.R., N.L. Herndon, S.L. Schulz, and J.E. Darroch. (2004), *Our Voices, Our Lives, Our Futures: Youth and Sexually Transmitted Diseases.* Chapel Hill, NC: School of Journalism and Mass Communication, University of North Carolina at Chapel Hill.

Centers for Disease Control, (2000), Division of STD Prevention, *Sexually transmitted disease surveillance, 1999*, Atlanta: Department of Health and Human Services.

Department of Health and Human Services, (2001), *The Surgeon General's Call to Promote Sexual Health and Responsible Sexual Behavior*, (DHHS publication), Washington, DC, (p. 1-33).

Dittus, P.J. and J. Jaccard. (2000), Adolescents' Perceptions of Maternal Disapproval of Sex: Relationship to Sexual Outcomes. *Journal of Adolescent Health*, 26, 268-278.

Donenberg, G.R., H.W. Wilson, E. Emerson, and F.B. Bryant. (2002), Holding the Line with a Watchful Eye: The Impact of Perceived Parental Permissiveness and Parental Monitoring on Risky Sexual Behavior Among Adolescents in Psychiatric Care. *AIDS Education and Prevention, 14* (2), 138-157.

Downie, N.M. & Heath, R.W. (1965), *Basic Statistical Methods, 2nd Ed.,* New York: Harper and Row.

Elliot, V.S. (2004), Studies Document High Rates of STDs Among Young People. *Amednews.com*, March 22. Retrieved May 18, 2004 (*http://www.ama-assn.org/amednews/2004/03/22/hlsd0322.htm*).

Emery, R.E. (1992), Family Conflicts and their Developmental Implications: A Conceptual Analysis of Meanings for the Structure of Relationships. In C.U. Shantz and W.W. Hartup (Eds.), *Conflict in Child and Adolescent Development.* New York: Cambridge University Press.

Field, T., C. Lang, R. Yando, and D. Bendell. (1995), Adolescents' Intimacy with Parents and Friends. *Adolescence, 30* (117), 133-141.

Frick, P.J. and Y.K. Jackson. (1993), Family Functioning and Childhood Antisocial Behavior: Yet Another Reinterpretation. *Journal of Clinical Child Psychology, 22* (4), 410-419.

Guttmacher Institute Report. (2004), *U.S. Teenage Pregnancy Statistics: Overall Trends, Trends by Race and Ethnicity, and State-by-State Information.* New York, NY: The Allen Guttmacher Institute.

The Center for Health and Health Care in Schools. (2004), Our Voices, Our Lives–A Report on Youth and STDs. *Health and Health Care in Schools, 5*(1). Retrieved May 19, 2004 from the CHHCS website (*http://www.healthinschools.org/ejournal/2004/mar1.htm*).

Harris, Kathleen Mullan, Francesca Florey, Joyce Tabor, Peter S. Bearman, Jo Jones, and J. Richard Udry. 2003 The National Longitudinal Study of Adolescent Health: Research Design [WWW document]. URL: http://www.cpc.unc.edu/projects/addhealth/design.

Hofferth, S.L., Kahn, J.R., Baldwin, W. (1987). Premarital sexual activity among US teenage women over the past three decades. *Family Planning Perspectives, 19*, 46-53.

Jaccard, J., P.J. Dittus, and V.V. Gordon. (2000). Parent-Teen Communication About Premarital Sex: Factors Associated with the Extent of Communication. *Journal of Adolescent Research, 15* (2), 187-208.

Kaplan, D.W., R.A. Feinstein, M.M. Fisher, J.D. Klein, L.F. Olmedo, E.S. Rome, et. al. (2001). Condom Use by Adolescents. *Pediatrics, 107* (6), 1463-1469.

Kiesler, D. J. (1983). The 1982 interpersonal circle: A taxonomy for complementarity in human transactions. *Psychological Review, 90,* 185-214.

Luster, T. and S.A. Small. (1994), Factors Associated with Sexual Risk-Taking Behaviors Among Adolescents. *Journal of Marriage and the Family, 56* (3), 622-633.

Maccoby, E.E., & Martin, J.A. 9 (1983), Socialization in the context of the family. In E.M. Hetherington (Ed.), *Handbook of child psychology.* New York: Wiley.

Majumdar, Debarun. Explaining Adolescent Sexual Risks by Race and Ethnicity: Importance of Individual, Familial, and Extra-familial Factors. *International Journal of Sociology of the Family*, 2005, 31 (1): 19-37.

Markham, C.M., S.R. Tortolero, S.L. Escobar-Chaves, G.S. Parcel, R. Harrist, and R.C. Addy. (2003), Family Connectedness and Sexual Risk-Taking Among Urban Youth Attending Alternative High Schools. *Perspectives on Sexual and Reproductive Health, 35* (4), 174-179.

Metzler, C.W. Noell, J., Biglan, A. & Ary, D., et. al. (1994). The Social Context for Risky Sexual Behavior Among Adolescents. *Journal of Behavioral Medicine, 17* (4), 419-438.

McLanahan, S., and Sanderfur, G. (1994), *Growing up with a single parent: What hurts, what helps.* Cambridge, MA: Harvard University Press.

Miller, B.C. (2002), Family Influences on Adolescent Sexual and Contraceptive Behavior. *Journal of Sex Research, 39* (1), 22-27.

Miller, K.S., R. Forehand, and B.A. Kotchick. (1999), Adolescent Sexual Behavior in Two Ethnic Minority Samples: The Role of Family Variables. *Journal of Marriage and the Family, 61* (1), 85-98.

Morrongiello, B.A. & Dawber, T. A. (1999), Parental Influences on Toddlers' Injury Risk Behaviors: Are Sons and Daughters Socialized Differently? *Journal of Applied Developmental Psychology, 20 (2),* 227-251.

Mosher, W. and McNally, J. (1991), Contraceptive use at First Premarital Intercourse: United States, 1965-1988. *Family Planning Perspectives, 23*, 108-116.

Perkins, D.F., T. Luster, F.A. Villarruel, and S. Small. (1998), An Ecological, Risk-Factor Examination of Adolescents' Sexual Activity in Three Ethnic Groups. *Journal of Marriage and the Family, 60* (3), 660-673.

Resnick, M.D., P.S. Bearman, R.Wm. Blum, K.E. Bauman, K.M. Harris, J. Jones, J. Tabor, T. Beuhring, R.E. Sieving, M. Shew, M. Ireland, L.H. Bearinger, and J.R. Udry. (1997). Protecting Adolescents from Harm: Findings from the National Longitudinal Study on Adolescent Health. *Journal of the American Medical Association, 278* (10), 823-832.

Rodgers, K.B. (1999). Parenting Processes Related to Sexual Risk-Taking Behaviors of Adolescent Males and Females. *Journal of Marriage and the Family 61* (1), 99-109.

Romer, D., Black, M., Ricardo, I., Feigelman, S., Kaljee, S., Galbraith, J., Nesbit, R., Horne, R.C., and Stanton, B. (1994). Social influences on the sexual behavior of youth at risk for HIV exposure. *American Journal of Public Health, 84,* 977-985.

Schaefer, E. S. (1959). A Circumplex Model for Maternal Behavior. *Journal of Abnormal and social Psychology, 59,* 226-235.

Small, S.A. and T. Luster. (1994a). Adolescent Sexual Activity: An Ecological, Risk-Factor Approach. *Journal of Marriage and the Family,56*, 181-192.

Small, S., Luster, T., (1994b).Factors associated with sexual risk-taking behaviors among adolescents. *Journal of Marriage and the Family, 56,* 622-632.

SPSS (1998). *SPSS Base 8.0: Applications Guide.* Chicago: SPSS Inc.

Udry, J. R. (2003) The National Longitudinal Study of Adolescent Health (Add Health), Waves I & II, 1994–1996 [machine-readable data file and documentation]. Chapel Hill, NC: Carolina Population Center, University of North Carolina at Chapel Hill.

Upchurch, D.M., C.S. Aneshensel, C.A. Sucoff, and L. Levy-Storms. (1999), Neighborhood and Family Contexts of Adolescent Sexual Activity. *Journal of Marriage and the Family, 61* (4), 920-933.

Weinstock, H., S. Berman, and W. Cates Jr. (2004), Sexually Transmitted Diseases Among American Youth: Incidence and Prevalence Estimates, 2000. *Perspectives on Sexual and Reproductive Health, 36*(1). Retrieved May 20, 2004 (*http://www.guttmacher.org/pubs/journals/3600604.html*).

Wilder, E.I. And T.T. Watt. (2002), Risky Parental Behavior and Adolescent Sexual Activity at First Coitus. *The Milbank Quarterly, 80* (3), 481-524.

Wu, L., and Martinson, B. (1993). Family structure and the risk of a premarital birth. *American Sociological Review, 58*, 210-232.

APPENDIX

Factor items	*Responses*	*Factor Loadings*
Father affect (5items)		
Overall, you are satisfied with the relationship with your father?[a]	Strongly agree–Strongly disagree	0.83
You are satisfied the way your father and you communicate with each other.[a]	Strongly agree–Strongly disagree	0.81
How close do you feel to your {father/adoptive father/stepfather/ foster father/etc.}?	Not at all-Very much	0.79
Most of the time, your father is warm and loving to you.[a]	Strongly agree–Strongly disagree	0.77
How much do you think he cares about you?	Not at all-Very much	0.64
Mother affect (10 items)		
Overall, you are satisfied with the relationship with your mother?	Strongly agree–Strongly disagree	0.81
You are satisfied the way your mother and you communicate with each other.	Strongly agree–Strongly disagree	0.79
How close do you feel to your {mother/adoptive mother/stepmother/ foster mother/etc.}?	Not at all-Very much	0.74
Most of the time, your mother is warm and loving to you.	Strongly agree-Strongly disagree	0.74
When you do something wrong that is important, your mother talks about it with you and helps you understand why it is wrong.	Strongly agree-Strongly disagree	0.69
Your mother encourages you to be independent.	Strongly agree-Strongly disagree	0.59
How much do you think she cares about you?	Not at all-Very much	0.54
How much do you feel that your family pays attention to you?	Not at all-Very much	0.48
How much do you feel that people in your family understand you?	Not at all-Very much	0.48

How much do you feel that you and your family have fun together?	Not at all-Very much	0.47

Appendix A (continued)
Parental Control (6 items)

Do your parents let you make your own decisions about:		
how much television you watch?	Yes/no	0.67
which television programs you watch?	Yes/no	0.65
what you wear?	Yes/no	0.59
what you eat?	Yes/no	0.54
what time you go to bed in weeknights?	Yes/no	0.53
the people you hang around with?	Yes/no	0.53

Parental Permissiveness (10 items)

How would mother feel about having sexual intercourse with someone who was special to you and whom you knew well–like a steady {girlfriend/boyfriend}?	Strongly disapprove-Strongly approve	0.79
How would she feel about your having sex at this time in your life?	Strongly disapprove-Strongly approve	0.79
How would father feel about having sexual intercourse with someone who was special to you and whom you knew well – like a steady {girlfriend/boyfriend}?	Strongly disapprove-Strongly approve	0.78
How would he feel about your having sex at this time in your life?	Strongly disapprove-Strongly approve	0.76
If you had sexual intercourse, it would upset your mother	Strongly agree-Strongly disagree	0.72
How would she feel about your using birth control at this time in your life?	Strongly disapprove-Strongly approve	0.61
How would he feel about your using birth control at this time in your life?	Strongly disapprove-Strongly approve	0.60
If R is male: If you got someone pregnant, it would be embarrassing to your family	Strongly agree-Strongly disagree	0.58

Appendix A (continued)

If R is female: If you got pregnant, it would be embarrassing to your family	Strongly agree-Strongly disagree	
If you had sexual intercourse.. afterward, you would feel guilty	Strongly agree-Strongly disagree	0.56
If R is male: If you got someone pregnant … it would be embarrassing for you.	Strongly agree-Strongly disagree	0.56
If R is female: If got someone pregnant… it would be embarrassing for you.	Strongly agree-Strongly disagree	

Source: Add Health Wave 1 (1995).
a. Items reverse coded

EXPLAINING ADOLESCENT SEXUAL RISKS BY RACE AND ETHNICITY

Debarun Majumdar

2

INTRODUCTION

The incidence of risky sexual activity and its negative consequences vary among adolescents belonging to different racial and ethnic groups in America (Miller, Norton, Curtis, Hill, Schvanneveldt, and Young, 1997; Upchurch et al., 1998). African American adolescents are more likely to commence sexual activity at earlier ages than other racial groups (Coker et al., 1994; Miller et al., 1997). They also have higher levels of sexually transmitted diseases (STDs) compared to Whites (Centers for Disease Control, 2001).

The rates of gonorrhea among African American and Hispanics adolescents were 24 and 12 times than that of Whites respectively (Panchaud, Singh, Feivelson, and Darroch, 2000; Department of Health and Human Services, 1998). Hispanics made for 19 per cent of the new HIV cases, whereas their population share is about 12 percent (Dailard, 2002).

Several studies have attempted to explain racial and ethnic variability in adolescent sexual activity and outcomes (Upchurch, Levy-Storms, Sucoff, and Aneshensel, 1998; Lauritsen, 1994; Furstenberg, Morgan, Moore, and Peterson, 1987). Furstenberg et al. (1987) found that extra-familial factors, such as racial composition of classroom and perceptions of sexual activity among peers mitigated the effects of race. Subsequent to Furstenberg et al.'s 1987 study, others have shown that some of the unexplained variability could be accounted for by family structure and neighborhood variables (Upchurch et al., 1998; Lauritsen 1994). Among female adolescents, family structure and neighborhood characteristics explained the race differences in sexual activity between Blacks and Whites (Lauritsen, 1994). Similarly Upchurch et al.'s (1998) study found that family background variables explained the racial differences in the timing of sexual activity for most race-gender combinations.

Even though family structure, neighborhood characteristics, racial composition of schools explain some of the racial disparity in sexual activity among adolescents, differentials in sexual behaviors still exist (Upchurch et al., 1998; Lauritsen, 1994; Furstenberg et al., 1987). Furtstenberg and colleagues (1987) contend that the unexplained variability is often mistakenly attributed to "cultural differences." However, the exact nature of "cultural differences" has not been clearly identified. This could be attributed to methodological issues and variables that have not been measured. In this research I examine factors that have not been previously explored to account for racial and ethnic differences in risky sexual activity among adolescents. These factors are distinguished at the individual, familial, and extra-familial levels.

Individual, Familial, and Extra-familial Factors

At the individual level, factors related to adolescent psychology and perceptions affect their chances of engaging in risky sexual behaviors (Resnick , Bearman, Blum, Bauman, Harris, Jones, Tabor, Beuhring, Sieving, Shew, Ireland, Bearinger, and Udry, 1997; St. Lawrence, Eldridge, Reitman, Little, Shelby, & Brasfield, 1998; Reitman, St. Lawrence, Jefferson, Alleyne, Brasfield, and Shirley, 1996). Individual factors such as depressive symptoms, self-efficacy, sexual risk-perceptions, and motivations to participate in risky behaviors may vary among different racial and ethnic groups. Teenagers suffering from depression are likely to engage in risky sexual activities such as not using condoms during sexual intercourse (Shrier, Harris, Sternberg, and Beardslee, 2001; Walter, Vaughan, and Cohall, 1995). Adolescents with high levels of self-efficacy and self-esteem may take precautionary measures against risky sexual behavior more successfully (Reitman et al., 1996; Luster and Small, 1994). Perception of sexual risk might determine the extent to which adolescents may engage in risky activities (Kotchick, Shaffer, Forehand, and Miller, 2001). Those who perceive themselves susceptible to unwanted outcomes like contracting STDs or untimely pregnancy may develop strategies that reduce such risks (Miller, Kotchick, and Forehand, 1999). Yet, from a cultural perspective, adolescents who belong to ethnic communities where teenage sexual activity is normative might be motivated to be sexually active. If sexual activity is perceived to bring respect or make someone more attractive, motivation to have sex or take sexual risks may be substantial (Furstenberg et al., 1987). Thus, the question is after accounting for the explanations at the individual level, are the racial and ethnic disparities in risky sexual activities eliminated?

Past literature provides ample evidence of the relationship between family processes like parental monitoring, connectedness, involvement, and sexual values and risky behaviors including risky sexual activity among teenagers (Wilder and Watt, 2002; Markham, Tortolero, Escobar-Chavez, Parcel, Harrist, and Addy, 2003; Small and Luster, 1994a,b; Miller, Forehand, and Kotchick, 1999; Newcomer and Udry, 1984). In these studies the role of family processes in understanding racial disparity in risky sexual activity has not been sufficiently examined. When adolescents perceive that their parents hold permissive sexual values, they are more likely to take sexual risks (Jaccard and Dittus, 2000). Studies such as Billy and Udry (1984), have indicated that Blacks hold permissive sexual values to a greater extent than Whites that could lead to participating in risky sexual behaviors. Upchurch et al. (1998) found that intact family structure explained the variation in age of sexual debut for Hispanics and Asians compared to their White counterparts. They argue that families protect Asian and Hispanic adolescents from initiating sex at young ages. Family processes such as support and monitoring also differentiated between sexually experienced and inexperienced teens (Jaccard, Dittus, and Gordon, 1996; Small and Luster, 1994a, b). Although family processes are related to sexual behaviors, do they explain racial and ethnic differences in risky sexual activity?

Extra-familial factors such as peers and neighborhood quality also affect sexual activity among adolescents (Perkins, Luster, Villarruel, and Small, 1998; Brewster, 1994; Hogan and Kitagawa, 1985). Although peers' influence has been examined in prior studies, the effect of *best friends* on adolescent behavior is not known. Regnerus (2002) argues that the distinction between friends and peers should be made because, unlike peers, friends may have a protective effect on teenagers and can shelter them from harm. Delinquent friends may increase the chances of engaging in risky sexual activities (Brewster 1994; Metzler, Noell, Biglan, Ary, and Smolkowski, 1994). The relationship between peer delinquency and risky sexual activity may be more pronounced in racial and ethnic groups where sexual experience is considered normative (Perkins et al., 1998; Furstenberg et al., 1987). Furthermore, substantial neighborhood effects on teenage pregnancy and childbearing were found in Hogan and Kitagawa's (1985) research. Low neighborhood quality was associated with increased risk-taking among African American girls (Brewster, 1994). However it is unknown whether race or ethnicity continues to exert significant influence on risky sexual behavior among adolescents after adjusting for extra-familial factors?

This study builds on past research and focuses on explanations at the individual, familial, and extra-familial levels that may account for the differences in risky sexual activity among teenagers based on race and ethnicity. Specifically, after controlling for these factors, do racial and ethnic differences in risky sexual activity among adolescents continue to persist? Comparisons of sexual activity typically have been carried out between Blacks and Whites. This paper overcomes this drawback by including Latino and Asian groups along with Blacks and Whites. With the increase in minority ethnicities like Hispanics and Asians in the American population, it is imperative that adolescents belonging to these rapidly growing groups are also studied systematically. Furthermore, this study extends past research on teenage sexual behavior by focusing on *risky* sexual activities.

METHODS

Data and Sample

Data from the 1995 National Longitudinal Study of Adolescent Health (Add Health) is used for analysis. Add Health is a nationally representative dataset where information is collected using the clustered sampling procedure. This dataset primarily pertains to adolescent health issues and contains a broad array of information related to teenage sexual behaviors, their family, peers, relationships, community among other topics. The education level of the sample ranged between seventh and twelfth grade of schooling. The data used for this analysis were collected from in-home interviews that yielded a sample of 20,745 cases. Care was taken to record sensitive questions by having adolescents enter responses directly into a computer with the help of audio CASI (Computer-assisted self-interviewing). This reduced the chances of social desirability for responses and interviewer bias. A detailed description of the data and sampling methods can be found in Bearman et al., 1997. This study includes 8,274 adolescents who have had sexual intercourse at the time of the interview. The sample contains only sexually active individuals because they would have been exposed to some level of sexual risk that could have result in undesired outcomes such as contracting an STD or having an unwanted pregnancy (Markham et al., 2003; Bakken and Winter, 2002; Shrier, Harris, Sternberg, Beardslee, 2001; Whitaker; Miller, may, and Levin, 1999). This is the baseline sample before listwise deletion. The sample did not include adolescents younger than 11 years due to the possibility of childhood sexual abuse (Abma, Driscoll, and Moore, 1998; Hofferth, Kahn, and Baldwin, 1987).

Dependent Variables

Risky sexual behaviors: There are three outcome variables that indicate risky sexual behavior. The first variable is non-use of contraceptive methods during most recent intercourse. This variable overwhelmingly represents condom usage which is the method of choice for 85 per cent of the sample. The second variable is ever having had an STD, such as chlamydia, gonorrhea, syphilis, HIV/AIDS, genital herpes, genital warts, or trichomoniasis. The third variable indicates initiating sexual intercourse at a young age–14 years and under. The sample for this outcome variable includes adolescents who were at least 14 years old. These variables have been established as indicators of teenage sexual risk in prior studies, e.g., Wilder and Watt, 2002; Markham et al., 2003.

Key Independent Variables

Race and ethnicity. This variable is created from self-reported information on race and ethnicity. The recoded variable consists of Whites, Blacks, Hispanics, Asians, and other. The “other” racial category is omitted from the analysis because there were very few individuals (n=10) who were sexually active.

Self-efficacy. This scale indicates the degree of control adolescents exercise to protect themselves from sexual risks. The three items used are "If you wanted to use birth control, how sure are you that you could stop yourself and use birth control once you were highly aroused or turned on?", "How sure are you that you could plan ahead to have some form of birth control available?", "How sure are you that you could resist sexual intercourse if your partner did not want to use some form of birth control?" The responses ranged from "very sure" (1) to "very unsure" (5). The self-efficacy scale is created by reverse coding these items where high values indicate high levels of self-efficacy. The reliability of this scale is 0.61 indicating moderate internal consistency among the items.

Sexual risk perception. This two-item scale indicates the extent to which adolescents perceived themselves as vulnerable to unwanted sexual outcomes such as untimely pregnancy or acquiring an STD. The items are "Imagine that sometime soon you were to have sexual intercourse with someone just once, but were unable to use any method of birth control for some reason. What is the chance that you would get (If respondent is male, add: your partner) pregnant?", "Suppose that sometime soon you had sexual intercourse for a whole month, as often as you wanted to, without using any protection. What is the chance that you would get the AIDS virus?" The responses range from "almost no chance" (1) to "almost certain" (5). High scores indicated high levels of perception of individual sexual risk. The two items of this scale are significantly correlated to each other in the same direction with moderate strength ($r=0.32$, $p<0.001$)

Sexual motivation. This scale consists of 5 items that capture adolescents' motivations to have sex. These items reflect the extent to which adolescents perceive benefits of sexual activity. The items are "If you had sexual intercourse, your friends would respect you more", "If you had sexual intercourse, it would give you a great deal of physical pleasure", "If you had sexual intercourse, it would relax you", "If you had sexual intercourse, it would make you more attractive to women/men", "If you had sexual intercourse, you would feel less lonely." The responses range from "strongly agree" (1) to "strongly disagree" (5). The items are reverse coded and a summative scale is formed where high values indicate high motivations to have sex. The reliability of this scale is 0.77.

Depression Symptoms. A scale capturing symptomatology of depression experienced in the past week is created using 19 related items. These items are a modified version of the Center for Epidemiologic Studies Depression Scale (CES-D, Radloff, 1977). The following represents some items in this scale: "You didn't feel like eating, your appetite was poor", "You felt depressed", "You felt lonely", "It was hard to get started doing things." Four items captures positive feelings and are reverse coded. The responses range from "never or rarely" (0) to "most of the time or all of the time" (3). These values are rescaled to 1 through 4 in the same direction as the original values and the 19 items are summed to form a depression scale. High values indicate high levels of depressive symptomatology in the adolescents. The reliability of this scale is 0.86.

Parental support. This scale measures the degree of perceived emotional support received from both parents. The items related to this scale are asked separately of both parents. They are: "How close do you feel to your mother/father?", "Most of the time, your mother/father is warm and loving toward you?", "How much do you think she/he cares about you?" The responses of the first two items ranged from "not at all" (1) to "very much" (5). The responses of the third item ranged from "strongly agree" (1) to "strongly disagree" (5). The third item is reverse coded to form a summative scale where higher values indicate higher levels of parental support. The values of adolescents with two parents are averaged to make them comparable to those with single parents. The reliability of this scale is 0.79.

Parental involvement. Parental involvement in adolescents' life is determined from ten items that indicate participation in various activities and time spent with teenage children. The adolescents were asked if they did the following with their parents in the past four weeks: "went shopping", "played a sport", "went to a religious service or church related event", "talked about someone you're dating, or a party you went to", "went to a movie, play, museum, or concert, or sport event", "had a talk about a personal problem you were having", "had a serious argument about your behavior", "talked about your school work or grades", "worked on a project for school", or "talked about other things you're doing in school." These items are asked separately of mothers and fathers. Similar to the previous variable, the mean value on this variable for two parents are considered to make them at par with single parent families. The values of the responses are "no" (0) or "yes" (1). A summative scale was constructed where higher values indicate higher levels of parental involvement. The reliability of this scale is 0.72.

Parental sexual permissiveness. This scale is intended to capture permissive sexual values of parents as perceived by the adolescents. This scale is created from three items that relate to parental attitudes towards adolescent sexual activity asked separately of their mothers and fathers. They are: "how would s/he feel about your having sex at this time in your life?", "how would s/he feel about your having sexual intercourse with someone who was special to you and whom you knew well-like a steady (girlfriend/boyfriend)?", and "How would s/he feel about your using birth control at this time in your life?" The responses ranged from "strongly approve" (1) to "strongly disapprove" (5). The values were reverse coded and the scale ranged from 3 through 15 with high scores representing high levels of perceived permissive sexual attitudes of parents. The values for two parents are averaged to make them comparable to single parents. The reliability of this scale is 0.88.

Best friend interaction. This scale reflects the level of contact and communication adolescents have with their best friends. Five items are used to measure best friend interaction. They are if an adolescent "went to a friend's house during the past seven days", "met a friend after school to hang out or go somewhere during the past seven days", "spent time with a friend during the past weekend", "talked about a problem during the past seven days", or "talked to friend on the telephone during the past seven days." The values of the responses are "no" (0) or "yes" (1). The responses of the *best* male and *best* female friends from a list of five friends of each gender nominated by the adolescent are used. High scores indicate high levels of interaction with best friends. The reliability of this scale is 0.72.

Peer delinquency: Delinquency level of friends is measured from the following three questions asked of their three best friends: "how many smoked at least 1 cigarette a day", "how many drank alcohol at least once a month?", or "how many used marijuana at least once a month." A summative scale is developed with higher values indicating higher levels of peer delinquency. The reliability of this scale is 0.76.

Neighborhood quality. This scale includes items related to neighborhood safety and neighborliness. They are " Do you usually feel safe in your neighborhood" and "People in this neighborhood look out for each other" and "You know most of the people in your neighborhood" and "In the past month, you have stopped on the street to talk to someone who lives in your neighborhood." The responses for the first item were "yes" (1) and "no" (0). The remaining items whose responses are "true" (1) and "false" (2) are reverse coded. A summative neighborhood quality scale is formed where high values indicate high neighborhood quality. This reliability of this scale is 0.55.

Socio-demographic controls

Several socio-demographic control variables that are related to adolescent sexual activity are included in the multivariate analyses. They are gender, family structure, age, religiosity, and income. The gender variable consists of two categories: male and female. The family structure variable is recoded into four categories: two biological parents, two step parents, single parents, and others. Age is measured in years. Religiosity is measured from the question "How important is religion to you?" The responses range from very important (4) to not important at all (1). Persons who indicate having no religion are placed in the "not important at all" category. The natural log version of the household income variable is used in the multivariate analyses. The missing information on income is estimated using regression analysis. An OLS estimation model is developed using parental education, race/ethnicity, and family structure as predictors. This model is used to estimate the household income for the missing cases. The missing information on income and those who indicated "no religion" are flagged by two dummy variables in the multivariate analysis.

RESULTS

Statistical Analysis

Due to the complex nature of the clustered sample, STATA/SE software is used for statistical analysis. This software allows the weights to be applied to the sample cases to account for the design effects. Multiple logistic regression models are developed to examine the association between race and ethnicity and the dichotomous sexual risk outcome variables. Logistic regression is used due to the binary nature of the dependent variables. Three models are developed for each dependent variable and a specific sequence of entering the key independent variables and socio-demographic variables is followed. In Model I, the race and ethnicity variables are first entered. This model sometimes is referred to as the baseline model. Then the key independent variables, i.e., the individual factors, family process variables, and extra-familial factors, are added in Model II. This step determines if race and ethnicity effects are accounted for by the key independent variables. Separate analyses (not shown) are also performed to determine which block of independent variables explains the relationship between risky sexual behavior and race/ethnicity. This is accomplished by entering each block of individual, familial, and extra-familial factors separately to the baseline model. The socio-demographic controls are added in Model III, which is also referred to as the full model. It should be noted that the Asian racial category is not included in the model predicting STDs chances because a very small number (n=18) of individuals experienced the event.

Sample Characteristics

Descriptive statistics for the sexually active sample are shown in Table 1. Regarding risky behavior, about a third (33 per cent) of the sample did not use contraception during last sexual intercourse; about 7 per cent of the sample ever had an STD; and 35 per cent had sexual intercourse before the age of 14. The racial and ethnic composition of the sample was 62 per cent White, 24 per cent Black, 11 per cent Hispanic, and 2 per cent Asian. Males made up 53 per cent of the sample and females 47 per cent. About 41 per cent of the adolescents came from two-parents biological families, another 11 per cent from step families, 35 per cent from single-parent families, and the remaining from other family structures. The average age of the sample was 16.9 yrs and the level of religiosity was high (2.8 out of 4). The average household income level was $42,312. On the average, the level of self-efficacy was high (12.7 out of 15), level of perceiving being at sexual risk was moderate (6.5 out of 10), motivation to have sex was moderate (14.6 out of 25), and the

Table 1
Characteristics of Sample of Sexually Active Adolescents[1]

	Total Sample (N=8, 274)
Dependent Variables (per cent)[2]	
No Contraception	32.7
Ever had STD	7.3
Had sex before 14	35.2
Independent Variables	
Race / Ethnicity (per cent)	
White	61.8
Black	24.0
Hispanic	11.4
Asian	2.4
Other	0.2
Sociodemographic Controls	
Sex (per cent)	
Female	47.2
Male	52.8
Family structure (per cent)	
Two parent biological	41.1
Two parent step	11.3
Single parent	34.5
Other	13.0
Age *(years)*	16.9
Religiosity *(1-4)*[3]	2.8
Household income *('000s)*	42,312
Individual factors	
Self efficacy *(3-15)* [3]	12.7
Sexual risk perception *(2-10)* [3]	6.5
Sexual motivations *(5-25)* [3]	14.6
Depression *(19-76)* [3]	31.7
Family Processes	
Parental involvement *(0-10)* [3]	3.4
Parental support *(3-15)*[3]	13.4
Parental sexual permissiveness *(3-15)* [3]	8.2
Extra-familial factors	
Best friend interaction *(0-10)* [3]	6.2
Peer delinquency *(0-9)* [3]	4.0
Neighborhood quality *(0-4)* [3]	3.1
Dummy variables (per cent)	
Income	26.6
Religiosity	18.5

Source: Add Health Wave 1 (1995)

1. Percentages and means are weighted
2. Percentages where indicated, otherwise means
3. Value ranges in parentheses

adolescents exhibited low levels of depressive symptoms in the past week (31.7 out of 76). The adolescents indicated low levels of parental involvement (3.4 out of 10), high levels of parental support (13.4 out of 15), and perceived low levels of parental sexual permissiveness (8.2 out of 15). The mean level of best friend interaction was moderate (6.2 out of 10), peer delinquency was low (4 out of 10), and perception of neighborhood quality was high (3.1 out of 4).

The distribution of risky sexual behavior by race and ethnicity is presented in Table 2. Among the racial and ethnic groups, the percentage that failed to use contraception during recent sexual intercourse was highest among Asians (46 per cent) followed closely by Hispanics (42 per cent). Blacks (13 per cent) were most likely to have ever experienced an STD compared to Whites (5 per cent) or Hispanics (6 per cent). Almost half of Black and a third of sexually active White adolescents initiated sexual intercourse before the age of 14. The bivariate chi-square analyses of risky sexual behaviors and race and ethnicity were significant ($p<0.001$, Table 2). A combination of the indicators of risk shows that a considerable proportion of sexually active adolescents engaged in at least one risky sexual behavior. Among Asian, Black, and Hispanic adolescents almost 60 per cent or more engaged in at least one risky sexual behaviors. For whites this was little more than half.

Table 2
Percentage distribution of risky sexual behavior by race and ethnicity[1]

	Dependent Variables			
	No contraception[2]	*Ever STD[2]*	*Sex before 14[2,3]*	*Some risk[4]*
Race/Ethnicity				
White	33.3[5]	5.0	30.1	51.9
Black	37.3	13.2	48.6	62.6
Hispanic	41.5	6.1	38.0	64.0
Asian	45.8	-[6]	33.4	59.1

Source: Add Health Wave 1 (1995)

1. Percentages are weighted.
2. $p<0.001$ for bivariate chi-square tests between dependent variables and race/ethnicity.
3. Sample restricted to 14 years and older.
4. Participated in at least one of the three indicators of sexual risk or two for Asians.
5. Among White adolescents, 33.3 per cent did not use any method at last sex.
6. Omitted because number of Asians adolescents with STDs in unweighted sample was low (n=18).

Sexual Risk and Race and Ethnicity

The results of the effect of race and ethnicity on specific sexual risks are presented in Table 3. Hispanic teenagers were 50 per cent more likely than Whites to not use any contraception during most recent sex (Model Ia). However, once the individual, familial, and extra-familial were added, the effect for Hispanics was no longer significant (Model IIa). The race and ethnicity variable continued to be non-significant after including the socio-demographic variables (Model IIIa). In a separate analysis (not shown) it was found that the block of individual factors accounted for the elevated odds of Hispanic adolescents not using contraception at most recent intercourse compared to Whites. Importantly, although the effects for Asians did not reach significance at a=0.05, they were marginally ($0.05<p<0.10$) about 50 per cent more likely not to use contraception compared to Whites. Blacks were not significantly different in their chances of not using contraception compared to Whites.

Sexually active African American adolescents were significantly more likely than Whites to have ever contracted an STD. This was evident in all models (Ib, IIb, IIIb, Table 3). The individual, familial, extra-familial factors or the socio-demographic variables did not eliminate the disparity between Blacks and Whites. In fact, after adjusting for the key independent variables and socio-demographic controls, Blacks were 200 per cent more likely to have had an STD compared to Whites (Model IIIb). Hispanics and Whites were no different in the odds of ever having had an STD.

African American and Hispanic adolescents were more likely to have initiated sexual activity before the age of 14 compared to Whites (Model Ic, Table 3). Whites and Asians were not significantly different from each other. After accounting for the individual, familial, and extra-familial factors, the effect for Hispanics disappeared (Model IIc). Separate analyses showed that individual and extra-familial factors accounted for the higher odds of early sexual activity among Hispanic teenagers compared to Whites (analyses not shown). After adjusting for all variables, Blacks were slightly more than 100 per cent likely to have initiated sexual intercourse before 14 years of age compared to Whites (Model IIIc, Table 3). Thus, neither the key independent variables nor the socio-demographic controls could explain why Black adolescents commenced sexual activity at earlier ages than Whites.

Table 3
Multivariate Logistic Regression Models Predicting odds of Risky Sexual Behaviors Among Adolescents

	No Contraception			*Ever had STD*			*Had sex before 14 years*[1]		
	Model Ia	*Model IIa*	*Model IIIa*	*Model Ib*	*Model IIb*	*Model IIIb*	*Model Ic*	*Model IIc*	*Model IIIc*
Independent Variables									
Race/Ethnicity									
Black	1.04	1.08	0.97	2.65***	4.16***	3.63***	2.18***	2.36***	2.08***
Hispanic	1.51***	1.23	1.21	1.03	1.23	1.22	1.36*	1.29	1.28
Asian	1.53	1.46	1.53	-[3]	-[3]	-[3]	1.09	1.27	1.36
White[2]	-	-	-	-	-	-	-	-	-
Individual factors[4]									
Self efficacy		0.85***	0.84***		1.02	0.97		0.95*	0.98
Sexual risk perception		0.90***	0.89***		0.99	0.97		0.94**	0.96*
Sexual motivations		0.97*	1.00		0.95*	1.02		1.03	1.01
Depression level		1.03***	1.02***		1.04***	1.02**		1.01	1.01
Family Process[4]									
Parental involvement		0.97	0.96		1.03	1.02		0.97	0.93**
Parental support		1.01	1.03		0.93	0.94		1.00	0.99
Parental sexual permissiveness		0.95***	0.96**		1.09**	1.11***		1.05**	1.05**
Extra-familial factors[4]									
Best friend interaction		0.97	0.97		1.06	1.04		0.96*	0.99
Peer delinquency		1.06***	1.05***		1.13***	1.15***		1.07***	1.08***
Neighborhood quality		0.91*	0.92		0.84**	0.89		1.01	0.99
Sociodemographic Controls									
Sex									
Female			1.71***			4.25***			0.71***
Male[2]			-			-			-
Family structure									
Two parent step			1.17			1.02			1.40*

Table 3 contd.

	No Contraception			*Ever had STD*			*Had sex before 14 years*[1]		
	Model Ia	*Model IIa*	*Model IIIa*	*Model Ib*	*Model IIb*	*Model IIIb*	*Model Ic*	*Model IIc*	*Model IIIc*
Single parent			1.06			1.11			1.71***
Other			1.07			1.66**			1.89***
Two biological parents[2]			-			-			-
Age			1.01			1.36***			0.72***
Religiosity[4]			1.02			1.15			1.07
Household income (log)[4]			0.86*			0.92			0.95
Missing dummies									
Income			1.15			1.28			0.90
Religiosity			1.26			1.45			1.08
F	4.00	13.85	11.06	28.54	14.21	13.17	13.29	10.46	12.73
N	7344	5339	5302	7466	5101	5063	6550	4923	4887

Source: Add Health Wave 1 (1995) **p*=0.05 ***p*=0.01 ****p*=0.001

1. Sample restricted to 14 years and older
2. Reference category
3. Omitted because number of Asians adolescents with STDs in unweighted sample was low (n=18)
4. Higher values indicate higher levels of the variables

Other Multivariate Findings

Among the individual factors, self-efficacy, perceptions of sexual risk, and depressive symptoms were associated with not using contraception net of the socio-demographic controls (Model IIIa). High levels of self-efficacy and perception of being at sexual risk reduced the odds of not using contraception. Increased depressive symptoms increased the odds of not using contraception and ever having had STDs (IIIa, b). The odds of participating in sexual activity before the age of 14 were reduced with higher levels of perceiving of being at sexual risk (IIIc). With respect to the family process variables, high levels of perceiving parents to be sexually permissive decreased the odds of not using contraception among adolescents, increased the odds of ever having had STDs, and also increased the same for having intercourse at a young age (IIIa, b, c). Parental involvement reduced the odds of early sexual activity (Model IIIc). Among the extra-familial variables, peer delinquency increased the odds of being at risk for all the three risk indicators (Models IIIa, b, c). The dummy variables were not predictive of any risky sexual behavior. This indicates that those who were missing in the information on income and religiosity were no different in their sexual risk propensities than their counterparts with valid responses.

DISCUSSION

This study shows that higher percentage of sexually active Hispanic and Asian adolescents did not use any contraception during most recent intercourse compared to Blacks or Whites. This is consistent with past research that found Hispanic adolescents having the lowest levels of condom utilization (Murphy and Boggess, 1998; Bankole, Darroch, and Singh, 1999). Although previous research considers Asian adolescents at very low sexual risk (Upchurch et al., 1998), this study shows that they have the highest percentage of not using contraception among all the race/ethnicity categories. Slightly higher percentage of Asians also appears to have initiated sexual intercourse at a young age compared to Whites. These findings are important because of two reasons. First, Asians are one of the fastest growing racial groups in the US with a relatively young age structure. Second, although they are considered to be at relatively low risk, this study clearly indicates that a substantial percentage of them are not using contraception, which makes them vulnerable to STDs and teenage pregnancy. The reluctance in using contraception may be explained by cultural factors where using or carrying contraception may bear the stigma of sexual stereotypes. It is also evident from this study that African American adolescents have the highest STD level compared to adolescents of other races and ethnicities. Additionally, Black adolescents were also most likely to have initiated sexual intercourse before 14 years. These results are consistent with past research, e.g., (Upchurch et al., 1998; Coker et al, 1994; Lauritsen 1994; Miller et al., 1997). Yet, this study also shows that at least half of the sexually active adolescents engaged in some risky sexual activities. In fact, for minorities this percentage is as high as 60 per cent.

Previous research indicated that family structure and neighborhood characteristics were possible explanations of racial differences in sexual behavior among adolescents (Lauritsen 1994; Upchurch et al., 1998). In addition, the current study found that individual and extra-familial factors could eliminate racial differences in risky sexual activity. Individual factors eliminated the differentials among Whites and Hispanics in the odds of not using contraception. Furthermore, individual and extra-familial factors eliminated racial and ethnic differences among Whites and Hispanics in the odds of initiating sexual intercourse at young ages. In fact, supplementary analysis showed that the mean level of self-efficacy is significantly higher for Whites than Hispanics ($p<0.01$). It is important to understand why Whites have higher levels of self-efficacy relative to Hispanics due to its important programme implications. Further analysis indicated that White adolescents have significantly higher levels of parental approval of contraceptive use compared to their Hispanic counterparts ($p<0.001$), which could lead to higher self-efficacy among Whites. This could explain the higher odds of not using contraception among Hispanics compared to Whites due to lower levels of parental approval. This suggests that programmes aimed at reducing unwanted sexual outcomes among Hispanic adolescents may target their parents in educating their children about contraception so that if their children engage in sexual activity then they have the knowledge to protect themselves. Additionally, once interaction with best friends was accounted for in the block of extra-familial variables, the elevated odds of Hispanic teenagers initiating sex at an early age compared to Whites disappeared (analyses not shown). White teenagers significantly had higher levels of interaction with their best friends ($p<0.001$). Interaction with best friends appears to reduce the odds of initiating early sex. Close friendship networks have been shown to protect adolescents from undesired behaviors such as using alcohol and chewing tobacco (Maxwell, 2002). Networks of close friends may protect teenagers from risky behaviors by increasing conformity to conventional behaviors. Programmes seeking to reduce teenage sexual risks may also encourage Hispanic adolescents to be a part of close friendship networks, which could shelter them from engaging in risky sexual behaviors. Thus, broadly, these factors indicate that specific explanations of race-ethnic differentials can be determined instead of relying on a "balance" cultural explanation, especially for the Hispanic-White case.

In line with past studies, such as Lauritsen, 1994 and Upchurch et al., 1998, this paper found that Black adolescents continued to be at greater sexual risk after adjusting for all key independent and socio-demographic variables. None of the variables at the individual, familial, or extra-familial levels eliminated the racial disparities in risky sexual behaviors between Blacks and Whites. Some possible reasons for this may be ineffective use of contraception (Fu, Darroch, Haas, and Ranjit, 1999) and having multiple sexual partners (Anderson and Dahlberg, 1992; Durbin et al., 1993). Some of the subgroup attitudes and norms towards early sexual activity may be explanations why Blacks are more likely to commence sexual activity before the age of 14 years than Whites. Further research needs to be conducted to determine explanations for the disparity in sexual risks between Blacks and Whites. Even if these differentials arise due to cultural factors, those factors need to be clearly identified.

There are several limitations of this study. Due to the cross-sectional nature of the data, there are issues related to the temporal order of the dependent and independent variables. This issue should be kept in mind while interpreting the results of this study. This is a disadvantage of using cross-sectional data and precludes the establishment of any causal relationships. This problem was also identified in the Shrier et al. (2001) and Wilder and Watt (2002) articles that used the ADD Health (1995) data. Instead of drawing causal inferences focus should be placed on associations between the dependent and independent variables. The data on risky sexual behavior are self-reported and thus, may be over-reported or under-reported. The STD variable was based on the diagnosis of a doctor or a nurse. Thus, adolescents who did not seek medical attention did not report contracting an STD, in spite of fact that they may have been infected (Shrier et al., 2001). Additionally, this study did not employ school level variables. Although, the information on peers may indirectly capture effect of school socialization, no direct measures were used. In spite of the attempt, this research also did not adequately provide explanations for the high likelihood of participating in sexual risks among Blacks. Although the self-efficacy and neighborhood quality scales are retained in the analyses due to their relevance, the internal consistency of the items assessing these scales is low. Finally, due to the limited number of Asian teenagers who ever experienced STDs, they were eliminated from the analyses. This racial group needs to be oversampled in future surveys because sufficient attention has not been paid to their sexual behaviors.

In summary, this study demonstrates that adolescents belonging to minority groups participate in risky sexual behaviors at greater levels than their White peers. Factors mostly at the individual and extra-familial levels provide explanations for differences in risky sexual activities between Whites and Hispanics. Overall, self-efficacy, perception of being at sexual-risk may reduce the likelihood of risky sexual behavior among adolescents, while perceived sexual permissive values of parents and depressive symptoms may increase the likelihood. More research needs to be conducted to fully understand why Black adolescents are at higher sexual risk than their counterparts in other racial and ethnic groups.

The author wishes to thank Dr. Toni Watt, Department of Sociology, Texas State University, and the anonymous reviewers for their invaluable suggestions on previous versions of this paper. He can be reached at dm28@txstate.edu.

REFERENCES

Abma, J.C., Driscoll, A., Moore, K. (1998). Young Women's Degree of Control over First Intercourse: An Exploratory Analysis. *Family Planning Perspectives,* 30, 12-18.

Anderson, J.E., and Dahlberg, L.L. (1992). High-Risk Sexual Behavior in the General Population: Results from a National Survey, 1988-1990. *Sexually Transmitted Diseases,* 19, 329-325.

Bakken, R.J and Winter, M. (2002). Family Characteristics and Sexual Behaviors among Black Men in the United States. *Perspectives on Sexual Reproductive Health,* 34, 252.

Bankole, A., Darroch, J.E., Singh, S. (1999). Determinants of Trends in Condom use in the United States, 1988-1995. *Family Planning Perspectives,* 31, 264-271.

Bearman PS, Udry, JR, The National Longitudinal Study of Adolescent Health: Research Design [WWW Document], 1997.

URL: http://www.cpc.unc.edu/projects/addhealth/design.html

Brewster, K. (1994). Race Differences in Sexual Activity among Adolescent Women: The Role of Neighborhood Characteristics. *American Sociological Review,* 59, 408-424.

Coker A.L., Richter D.L., Valois R.F., McKeown R.E., Garrison C.Z., & Vincent M.L. (1994). Correlates and Consequences of Early Initiation of Sexual Intercourse. *Journal of School Health,* 64, 372-377.

Dailard, C. (2002). Family Planning Clinics and STD Services. The Guttmacher Report on Public Policy, 5, 8-11.

Demuth, S., and Brown, S.L. (2004). Family Structure, Family Processes, and Adolescent Delinquency: the Significance of Parental Absence versus Parental Gender. *Journal of Research in Crime and Delinquency,* 41, 58-81.

Durbin M., DiClemente R.J., Siegel D., Krasnovsky F., Lazarus N., & Camacho T. (1993). Factors Associated with Multiple Sex Partners among Junior High School Students. *Journal of Adolescent Health,* 14, 202-207.

Fu, H., Darroch, J.E., Haas, T., Ranjit, N. (1999). Contraçeptive Failure Rates: New Estimates from the 1995 National Survey of Family Growth. *Family Planning Perspectives,* 31, 56-63.

Furstenberg, F.F., Morgan, S.P., Moore, K.A., & Peterson, J.L. (1987). Race Differences in the Timing of Adolescent Intercourse. *American Sociological Review,* 52, 511-518.

Hofferth, S.L., Kahn, J.R., Baldwin, W. (1987). Premarital Sexual Activity among US Teenage Women over the Past Three Decades. *Family Planning Perspectives,* 19, 46-53.

Hogan, D.P. and Kitagawa, E. M. (1985). The Impact of Social Status, Family Structure, and Neighborhood on the Fertility of Black Adolescents. *American Journal of Sociology,* 90, 825-855.

Jaccard, J., Dittus, P., Gordon, V. (2000). Parent-Teen Communication about Premarital Sex: Factors Associated with the Extent of Communication. *Journal of Adolescent Research,* 15, 187-208.

Jaccard, J., Dittus, P.J., Gordon, V.V. (1996). Maternal Correlates in Adolescent Sexual Behavior. *Family Planning Perspectives,* 28, 159-165.

Kotchick, B. A., Schaffer, A., Forehand, R., Miller, & Kim. S. (2001). Adolescent Sexual Risk Behavior: A Multi-System Perspective. *Clinical Psychology Review,* 21, 493-519.

Lauritsen, J.L. (1994). Explaining Race and Gender Differences in Adolescent Sexual Behavior. *Social Forces,* 72, 859-884.

Li X., Feigelman S., Stanton B. (2000). Perceived Parental Monitoring and Health Risk Behaviors among Urban Low-Income African-American Children and Adolescents. *Journal of Adolescent Health,* 27, 43-48.

Maxwell, K.A, (2002). "Friends: The Role of Peer Influence Across Adolescent Risk Behaviors." *Journal of Youth and Adolescence,* 31, 267-277.

Markham, C.M., S.R. Tortolero, S.L. Escobar-Chaves, G.S. Parcel, R. Harrist & R.C. Addy. (2003). Family Connectedness and Sexual Risk-Taking Among Young Urban Youth Attending Alternative High Schools. *Perspectives on Sexual and Reproductive Health,* 35, 174-179.

Metzler, C.W., Noell, J, Biglan, A. (1992). The Validation of a Construct of High-Risk Sexual Behavior in Heterosexual Adolescents. *Journal of Adolescent Research,* 7, 233-249.

Miller, K., Forehand, R., Kotchick, B. (1999). Adolescent Sexual Behavior in Two Ethnic Minority Samples: The Role of Family Variables. *Journal of Marriage and the Family,* 61, 85-98.

Miller, B.C., Norton, M., Curtis, T., M.C., Hill, E.J, Schvaneveldt, P., & Young, M.H. (1997). The Timing of Sexual Intercourse among Adolescents: Family, Peer, and other Antecedents. *Youth and Society,* 29, 54-83.

Murphy, J.J., and Boggess, S. (1998). Increased Condom use among Teenage Males, 1988-1995: The Role of Attitudes. *Family Planning Perspectives,* 30, 276-280.

Newcomer S.F., and Udry, J. R. (1984). Mother's Influence on the Sexual Behavior of their Teenage Children. *Journal of Marriage and the Family,* 46, 477-485.

Panchaund, C., Singh, S., Feivelson, D., & Darroch, J.E. (2000). Sexually Transmitted Diseases among Adolescents in Developed Countries. *Family Planning Perspectives,* 32, 24-32 & 45.

Perkins, D., Luster, T., Villarruel, F. (1998). An Ecological, Risk-Factor Examination of Adolescent's Sexual Activity in Three Ethnic Groups. *Journal of Marriage and the Family,* 60, 660-673.

Radloff, L. (1977). The CES-D Scale: A Self-Report Depression Scale for Research in the General Population. *Applied Psychological Measurement,* 1, 385-401.

Regnerus, M.D. (2002). Friends' Influence on Adolescent Theft and Minor Delinquency: A Developmental Test of Peer-Reported Effects. *Social Science Research,* 31, 681-705.

Reitman, D., St. Lawrence, J.S., Jefferson, K.W., Alleyne, E., Brasfield, T.L., & Shirley, A. (1996). Predictors of African American Adolescents' Condom Use and HIV Risk Behavior. *AIDS Education and Prevention,* 8, 499-515.

Resnick M.D., Bearman, P.S., Blum, R.W., Bauman. K.E., Harris, K.M., Jones, J., Tabor, J., Beuhring, T., Sieving, R.E., Shew, M., Ireland, M., Bearinger, L.H. & Udry, R.J. (1997). Protecting Adolescents from Harm: Findings from the National Longitudinal Study on Adolescent Health. *Journal of the American Medical Association,* 278, 823-832.

St. Lawrence, J.S., Eldridge, G.D., Reitman, D., Little, C.E., Shelby, M.C., & Brasfield, T.L. (1998). Factors Influencing Condom Use among African American Women: Implications for Risk Reduction Interventions. *American Journal of Community Psychology,* 26, 7-28.

Shrier L.A., Harris, S.K., Sternberg, M., & Beardsless, W.R. (2001). Associations of Depression, Self-Esteem, and Substance Use with Sexual Risk among Adolescents, *Preventive Medicine,* 33, 179-189.

Small, S., and Luster, T., (1994a). Factors Associated with Sexual Risk-Taking Behaviors among Adolescents. *Journal of Marriage and the Family,* 56, 622-632.

Small, S., and Luster, T. (1994b). Adolescent Sexual Activity: An Ecological, Risk-Factor Approach. *Journal of Marriage and the Family,* 56, 181-192.

Upchurch, D.M., Levy-Storms, L., Sucoff, C.A., & Aneshensel, C.S. (1998). Gender and Ethnic Differences in the Timing of the First Sexual Intercourse. *Family Planning Perspectives,* 30, 121-127.

Walter, H., Vaughan, R., Cohall, A. (1991). Psychosocial Influences on Acquired Immunodeficiency Syndrome-Risk Behaviors among High School Students. *Pediatrics,* 88, 846-52.

Wilder E.I. and Watt T.W. (2002). Risky Parental Behavior and Adolescent Sexual Activity at First Coitus. *The Milbank Quarterly,* 80, 481-524.

GENDER AND ETHNIC VARIATION IN LOVE MARRIAGE IN URBAN MALAYSIA

3

Xiaowei Zang

INTRODUCTION

Existing studies show that both the Malays and the Chinese relied on parental arrangement and free choice in pre-1990 Malaysia. However, the Malays reported a greater preference for arranged marriage than the Chinese, whereas the Chinese claimed a sizable advantage over the Malays in free choice. The inter-group variations were attributed mainly to Malay culture and ethnic disparity in status attainment (Hirschman and Teerawichitchainan, 2003; Jones, 1994; Leete, 1994; 1996). Do these two ethnic groups still differ from each other in free choice in the post-1990 era? If the answer is yes, are Malay culture and ethnic disparity in status attainment still the main determinants of the inter-group difference in marriage in Malaysia?

These questions are discussed in this paper with data collected from a mass survey (n = 1,967) conducted in Kuala Lumpur in 2002. This paper first reviews the post-1957 socio-demographic transition in Malaysia and the existing studies that explain inter-group variation in marriage in Islamic Southeast Asia in terms of Malay culture and status attainment. It then presents a gendered explanation of inter-group differences in free choice in the post-1990 era. Next, it discusses the data and major findings from data analysis. This paper concludes with a discussion of the gender effect on ethnic differences in marriage in Malaysia.

SOCIO-DEMOGRAPHIC CHANGES IN PRE-1990 MALAYSIA

Malaysia is a multiethnic country. Its official religion is Islam. Malay Muslims and the Chinese are two major ethnic groups in

Malaysia. They differ from each other in many aspects such as population size and religion. According to the Department of Statistics Malaysia, of the total population of Malaysia in Census 2000, the Malays comprised 65.1 percent, whereas the Chinese consisted of 26 percent. Virtually all the Malays are Muslims, while the vast majority of the Chinese are either atheists or practise other religions such as Buddhism, Taoism, Christianity, etc. The Malays are officially defined as the indigenous people of Malaysia (*bumiputeras*, i.e. sons of the land) and are rewarded with affirmative action benefits. In comparison, the Chinese are considered by the Malays as migrants. In fact, some of the Malays are recent migrants from Indonesia, while many Chinese are the second or third generation descendents of the early migrants from South China (Andaya and Andaya, 2001; Hamayotsu, 2002; Kheng, 2002; Martinez, 2002).[2]

When Malaysia gained independence in 1957, the Malay population was mainly rural and agrarian, while many Chinese were urban residents and engaged in commerce and handicraft. There was thus ethnic inequality in education, income, factory employment between the Malays and the Chinese before 1970. Government attempts to address this issue were largely unsuccessful. Consequently, a bloody clash between these two groups took place in 1969 right after an ethnically colored and hotly contested election campaign (Andaya and Andaya, 2001; Kheng, 2002). As a result, the Malaysian government implemented the New Economic Policy (NEP) in 1970 to reduce ethnic tension and inequality in education and occupational attainment. It provided opportunities and privileges for the Malays to start a private business, receive higher education, and work in modern economic sectors, often at the expense of other ethnic groups such as the Chinese. These affirmative action programs and the rapid economic growth since the 1970s have greatly enhanced Malay attainment in urban residence, education, and factory and professional employment (Koon, 1997; Raslan, 1996; Selvaratnam, 1988; Sudha, 1997).

It is necessary to point out that although many Chinese did not directly benefit from and might not be happy about the NEP, they have gained good profits from the economic boom since the 1970s. This is because they have been a major player in Malaysia's industrialization and the global trading system. Wealth has created affordability of higher education in Western countries for the children of middle-class and wealthy Malaysian Chinese (Holland, 2001; Koon, 1997; Yeung, 2000). Thus, the NEP and Malaysia's booming economy since the 1970s have "completely transformed the economic and social settings" in that country and the ways the Malays and the Chinese live everyday life (Leete, 1994: 811; also Jones, 1994; Leete, 1996). Scholars have found evidence of a rapid demographic transition in pre-1990 Malaysia (Caldwell, 1996: vii; Jones, 1994; Leete, 1996). One of the well-documented changes was mate selection. Leete (1994: 811, 815) finds "ever-decreasing proportions among younger generations entering into marriages arranged by their parents." In particular, since the 1950s, more and more Chinese women in Malaysia married the men of their own choices (Leete, 1994; 1996).

Changes in mate selection among the Malays were similarly impressive. Malay families traditionally arranged the marriage partners for their daughters, often before girls were 15 years old. Many scholars have argued that the main trend since the 1950s was the change "from a pattern of fairly tight control over adolescent females and universal, early, or parent-arranged marriages to one of freer female adolescence, much later, self-arranged marriage" among the Malays (Jones, 1981: 256; Jones, 1994: 16, 131, 144; Leete, 1994: 811, 815; also Heaton et al., 2001; Hirschman and Teerawichitchainan, 2003; Strange, 1976). The pre-1990 demographic transition was accompanied by a salient Malay-Chinese variation in marriage. For example, Chinese women claimed an advantage in free choice over their Malay sisters in every age group. In 1981, for example, 14 percent of Malay women aged 45 and above reported love marriages, as compared with 48 percent of the Chinese women in the same birth cohort (Jones, 1994: 134). Chinese women also differ from Malay women greatly in terms of fertility and age at marriage (Jones, 1994; also Leete, 1994; Morgan et al., 2002; Sudha, 1997).

EXISTING EXPLANATIONS OF ETHNIC VARIATION IN MARRIAGE

Many scholars have explained the ethnic variation in marriage mainly as the outcome of and cited it as evidence of the resilient effect of Malay culture on Malay marital behavior. Indeed, they find significant Malay-Chinese differences in marriage between the 1940s and the 1960s, even with key variables controlled in multivariate analysis (Brien and Lillard, 1994: 1,185-6;

Hirschman and Teerawichitchainan, 2003: 244; also Anderson et al., 1987; Heaton et al., 2001; Jones, 1981; 1997; Leete, 1994). Jones (1994: 115-6) explicitly argues that "In the area of marriage and divorce, cultural traditions with the sanction of religion held sway." In addition, some scholars have considered ethnic inequality as another major cause of the pre-1990 ethnic differences in marriage. They have described the Chinese as a more modern group than the Malays since the former had greater urban experience and reported a higher level of status attainment than the latter did (Jones, 1981: 256; also Hirschman and Teerawichitchainan, 2003; Jones, 1994). In fact, Leete (1994: 812-3) finds that "by 1990 Chinese women were on average aged around 26 years at the time of first marriage—slightly later than the corresponding age in much of Europe." The marriage patterns of Malaysian Chinese women form a sharp contrast to traditional marital behavior of Malay women at that time.

These scholars have also suggested an increasing impact of status attainment on Malay marriages. Jones (1981: 256) is perhaps the first scholar that projected this trend (also Heaton et al., 2001; Mabry, 1998). Hirschman and Teerawichitchainan (2003: 245) similarly state that traditional Malay marriage patterns may begin to erode with the spread of education in Islamic Southeast Asia since the 1960s. As "Western cultural values, including an emphasis on individualism, have deepened their hold in popular imagination around the world, the future of marriage and the family in Southeast Asia is uncertain."

GENDER AND ETHNIC DIFFERENCES IN FREE CHOICE

In short, existing studies suggest that Malay culture and ethnic variation in status attainment are two key determinants of Malay-Chinese differences in pre-1990 marriage patterns. This paper seeks to extend this insight by introducing gender into research on Malay culture, ethnic disparity, and marriage in the post-1990 era. This endeavor is based on an assumption that the effects of culture and ethnic disparity are not evenly distributed in a population. Many scholars point out that modernization is both an economic program and a cultural model/ or the way of life. A demographic transition occurs when this cultural model is adopted by the bulk of a population. For example, Alex Inkeles's notion of "modem man" reflects both the modernization forces and cultural changes that may have implications for marriage (Fong, 2004: 3; Goode, 1963; Inkeles, 1969; Rindfuss et al., 2004).

It is important to note that the degree and speed of the internalization of the cultural model in a population may vary greatly as individuals may adopt different responses to the family revolution due to their unique subjectivities and experiences (Fong, 2004). This paper focuses on one of these subjectivities and experiences, i.e. gender, to understand the effects of Malay culture and status attainment on both Malay marital behavior and ethnic differences in marriage.[3] Gender is chosen because of its prominent role in the Islamic marriage institution. It is chosen also because gender effects have been noted in the existing studies. Finally, it is chosen because of gender inequality in education and employment that significantly affects marriage.

Firstly, as a rule, Islam supports in-group marriage. A union between a Muslim groom and a non-Muslim bride is sometimes tolerated if the bride is a Christian or a Jew. But a marriage between a Muslim bride and a non-Muslim groom is only possible if the groom converts to Islam.[4] In fact, such unions are strongly opposed since it not only dilutes Muslim blood purity but also may result in a loss of group members (i.e., the wife and children) if the husband does not become a Muslim. Muslim motherhood is regarded as a key safeguard of Islamic culture. Hence, the Muslim community generally supervises mate seekers' dating behavior. More importantly, it is mainly a parental responsibility to monitor children's spousal decisions (Carolan, 1999; Gillette, 2000; Haddad, 1991; Sherif, 1999). This may suggest the heavy parental involvement in children's marriages in general and in daughters' marital behavior in particular. Everything being equal, the degree of family influence on Malay men may be lower than that on Malay women.

Secondly, existing research has studied the effect of gender on marriage in Islamic Southeast Asia and provided indirect evidence that shows greater family influences on young Malay women than their Muslim brothers. Scholars have noted a large age difference between spouses among the Malays during the 1980s, which is consistent with another finding that many Malay women reported early marriages (Jones, 1994: 105-8; also Anderson et al., 1987; Leete, 1994). It is possible that these findings are the result of the different marriage processes with which the Malay men and their Muslim sisters seek a mate in the marriage market: large spouse age differences and a young age at marriage among Malay women suggest heavy parental involvement in daughters' marriages. In other words, Malay men may have more power than Malay women to make a marriage decision. Not surprisingly, Jones (1994: 120) suggests that young Malay men have somewhat more say in the choice of their spouse than do young Malay women.

Thirdly, Malay culture may affect Malay women more than Malay men also because of gender inequality in social status. Malay men have gained more benefits than Malay women in terms of education and employment opportunities (Blackburn et al., 2000; Seguino, 2000a; 2000b). They thus may have a greater power to make a spouse choice than their Malay sisters due to gender disparity in social status. Parents are less capable of controlling or influencing the marriage decisions of higher status children (who are likely to be men) than those of lower status children (who are likely to be women). Higher status brings about a higher level of resources and hence autonomy for children. Finally, gender inequality in status attainment itself suggests that Malay men may be less likely than their Muslim sisters to be subject to traditional rituals due to their differences in education and exposure to modernization experience such as work. Educational attainment and employment are conducive to free choice and love marriage.

It is possible that the degree of gender disparity in status attainment among the Malays may have been reduced significantly as more and more Malay women have received university education and obtained better jobs. Yet it takes time for Malay women to catch up with Malay men in educational opportunities and career mobility. It also takes time for Malay women to translate the effect of status attainment into the concrete patterns of marital behavior. Furthermore, the translation should be easier for Malay men than for Malay women since the former may be subject to less parental control than the latter as mentioned above. These possibilities thus suggest a stronger effect of Malay culture on Malay women than on Malay men.

Based on the above discussion, it is possible that Malay men and Malay women may respond differently to culture and status attainment, i.e., social status variables may affect Malay women less than Malay men, and Malay culture variables may affect

Malay men less than Malay women. These gendered contrasts may be less salient among the Chinese since, as noted above, Chinese women are reported to be as modern as European women in marriage behavior (Leete, 1994). Accordingly, there may be significant differences in marriage between Malay women and Chinese women but not between Malay men and Chinese men. This gendered variation may be a key factor responsible for the aggregate Malay-Chinese difference in free choice.

DATA AND VARIABLES

This paper studies the above mentioned possibilities with data from a mass survey on family life in Kuala Lumpur conducted in 2002. The survey was commissioned to a survey firm in Kuala Lumpur that had done surveys for some international agencies and multinational firms. I wrote the English version of the questionnaire, which was translated into a Malay and a Chinese version by trilingual experts in the firm. The three versions of the questionnaire were then given to a trilingual scholar for cross-examination. No major discrepancies were reported. Thirty interviewers (12 Malays and 18 Chinese), who had at least one-year fieldwork experience, were recruited and trained before the survey. During the survey, the Malay interviewers were allocated to predominantly Malay areas and Chinese interviewers to predominantly Chinese areas.

The survey sample was drawn from residents in the Kuala Lumpur/Petaling Jaya area.[5] A total of 150 clusters were randomly selected using postal codes in this region as the sampling frame. Households were then randomly selected within each cluster. Like virtually all other mass surveys conducted in Kuala Lumpur today, the interviewers were able to persuade only 30 percent of the sampled respondents to participate in the survey. My fieldwork experience suggests that more than 70 percent of the residents in unguarded residences granted the survey requests. However, access to the sampled respondents in guarded residences was extremely limited. In most cases, interviewers did not get the permission from the selected respondents to enter these buildings. Rejection was easy since they talked to interviewers via telephone. These people are generally wealthier than the dwellers in unguarded residences. Findings reported in this research should be read with caution since they may mainly represent the patterns of mate selection among middle and lower class people in the city. In all, 2,005 respondents (Malays = 1,014 and Chinese = 991) were interviewed about among other aspects of life their socioeconomic attributes and marital histories. The cases with missing data are excluded from data analysis, which results in the final sample of 1,967 cases, with 994 being Malays and 973 being Chinese.

The dependent variable used in data analysis is *free choice*, which is a dummy variable—love marriages are coded as 1 and others as 0. In many Asian societies, free choice marriage does not necessarily mean children's total freedom in mate selection. Also, there is more of a continuum of arrangements such as matchmaking, introduction by parents, relatives, etc that lead to marriage (Tan and Jones, 1990).[6] Nevertheless, many scholars have described the demographic transition in Islamic Southeast Asia partly with regard to the movement from "parent-arranged marriages to a free choice of spouse by the individual..." (Jones, 1981: 271; also Jones, 1994; Heaton et al., 2001). In addition, free choice marriages and other types of unions indicate the different levels of parental involvement in children's marriage decisions, which are important as they can produce significantly different marital outcomes for these two types of marriages (see Pimentel, 2000).

Data analysis in this paper relies on birth cohort, education, work, rural father, father education, and Malay ethnicity as the independent variables. These variables are derived from the marital histories of the Kuala Lumpur respondents and measure retrospectively what they were *before the time of the marriage*.

Birth cohort. This is an ordinal variable with four levels: the first birth cohort includes those who were born before 1950; the second birth cohort, those who were born between 1950 and 1959; the third birth cohort, those who were born between 1960 and 1969; and the fourth birth cohort, those who were born after 1970. This measure has been a key variable in the studies of marriage in Southeast Asia since it can be used to observe the effect of modernization on marriage (Anderson et al., 1987; Brien and Lillard, 1994; Heaton et al., 2001; Hirschman and Teerawichitchainan, 2003).[7] Each succeeding birth cohort should have a higher degree of exposure to the influence of modernization and thus may report greater probabilities of free choice.

Education is an ordinal variable with the following six levels: (1) illiterate or semi-illiterate, (2) elementary school, (3) junior high school, (4) senior high school, (5) vocational school, and (6) university & above. This variable measures the educational levels of the respondents before marriage. Existing research shows a substantial effect of education on marriage patterns even with other key background characteristics controlled (Jones, 1994: 89-95, 100-2, 121, 154; also Heaton et al., 2001).

Many scholars also point out that work experience can increase the probabilities of late marriages and free choice in Southeast Asia (Anderson et al., 1987; Heaton, 1996; Leete, 1994). A dummy variable, *Worker*, is created to study the effect of employment on free choice marriage. A respondent is coded as 1 if he or she worked full time before the time of marriage and a part-time worker, a student, or a unemployed person is coded as 0. Another dummy variable, *Malay ethnicity* is created to measure the effect of Malay culture on free choice. The Malay respondents are coded as 1 and Chinese respondents as 0. Hirschman and Teerawichitchainan (2003: 216) suggest that Malay ethnicity can be used as a proxy for traditional Malay culture, which is thought to be a pervasive and persistent influence on marriage behavior.

Another measure of Malay culture is family background since higher status families may be less traditional than lower status households due to their differences in educational levels and occupational attainment. Many scholars hence consider family background a major variable in marriage decisions in Islamic Southeast Asia (Hirschman and Teerawichitchainan, 2003: 216; also Heaton et al., 2001; Jones, 1994). Two family background variables are used in this paper. First, *Rural father* is a dummy variable with the respondents whose fathers were rural farmers at the time of their marriages coded as 1 and others as 0. Second, *Father education* measures the educational levels of the respondents' fathers before their weddings. It is an ordinal variable with four levels: (1) illiterate or semi-illiterate, (2) elementary school, (3) junior high school, (4) senior high school & above.

FINDINGS

Table 1 shows some basic statistics of the Kuala Lumpur respondents. It seems that the two ethnic groups do not differ from each other greatly in terms of birth cohort and gender distributions. The percentage of workers among the Malays is also similar to that of the Chinese counterparts. However, the Malays attain a slightly higher level of educational attainment than the Chinese do. A possible explanation is the affirmative action policy for the Malays that may have eliminated the pre-1970 Chinese advantage in education. An additional explanation is the fact that Kuala Lumpur is the national capital of Malaysia with the heavy concentration of the Malay elites. National statistics on inter-group differences may show a different picture.

The same reasons may also explain why the fathers of the Malay respondents have the higher levels of educational attainments than their Chinese counterparts do. Again, national statistics on inter-group differences may show a different picture.[8] In addition, the percentage of the respondents whose fathers were a rural father is higher among the Malays than among the Chinese, which is consistent with the common knowledge that most Chinese have been urbanities whereas many Malays have moved to urban areas after 1970 in search of education and employment opportunities.

Table 1 also shows that each of the successive cohorts is more likely than its predecessor to use free choice to find a prospective mate in the marriage market. This is the case for both the Malays and the Chinese. However, the change is clearly more dramatic for the Malays than for the Chinese. Finally, Table 1 shows that over 60 percent of the marriages in Kuala Lumpur are based on free choice. Malay men report a slightly higher percentage of love marriages than Chinese men do. But this ethnic difference is not statistically significant. In comparison, Malay women are less likely than their Chinese sisters to report incidents of free choice. This ethnic difference is statistically significant.

The findings on inter-group differences in free choice reported in Table 1 are obtained without controls and do not show whether they are the outcomes of Malay culture or social status. Multivariate analysis is needed to see if they still exist with background characteristics being controlled and to identify the effects of Malay culture and social status on marriage. Two logistic regression analyses are performed on the Kuala Lumpur sample. Model 1 of Table 2 shows an upward trend in free choice among the Kuala Lumpur respondents. It seems that the more recent a marital union is formed, the more likely it is a love

Table 1
Descriptive Statistics

Characteristics	*Malays*	*Chinese*	*Kuala Lumpur*
Birth cohort (%)			
Before 1950	16.5 (164)	20.3 (198)	18.4 (362)
1950-1959	26.1 (259)	20.7 (201)	23.4 (460)
1960-1969	24.8 (247)	21.6 (210)	23.2 (457)
Born after 1970	32.6 (324)	37.4 (364)	35.0 (688)
Women (%)	49.0 (487)	52.7 (513)	50.8 (1,000)
Education (%)			
Below primary school	2.1 (21)	5.8 (56)	3.9 (77)
Primary school	13.4 (133)	23.9 (233)	18.6 (366)
Junior high school	21.4 (213)	21.2 (206)	21.3 (419)
Senior high school	40.9 (407)	31.7 (308)	36.3 (715)
Vocational school	3.5 (35)	2.7 (26)	3.1 (61)
University & above	18.6 (185)	14.8 (144)	16.7 (329)
Work (%)	74.4 (740)	73.3 (713)	73.9 (514)
Rural father (%)	26.9 (267)	15.4 (150)	21.2 (417)
Father education ((%)			
Below primary school	24.1 (240)	39.0 (379)	31.5 (619)
Primary school	46.1 (458)	39.6 (385)	42.9 (843)
Junior high school	14.3 (142)	11.7 (114)	13.0 (256)
Senior high school & above	15.5 (154)	9.8 (95)	12.7 (249)
Free choice by birth cohorts (%)			
Born before 1950	31.7 (52)	50.5 (100)	42.0 (152)
1950-1959	60.6 (157)	58.7 (118)	59.8 (275)
1960-1969	67.2 (166)	67.1 (141)	67.2 (307)
Born after 1970	71.3 (231)	67.3 (245)	69.2 (476)
Free choice by gender (%)			
Men	63.9 (324)	60.2 (277)	62.2 (601)
Women	57.9 (282)	63.7 (327)	60.9 (609)
N	994	973	1,967

Figures in the parentheses are numbers of cases.

marriage. However, the difference between the fourth birth cohort (the comparison group) and the third birth cohort is not statistically significant. Overall, these findings are consistent with those reported in the existing studies of Southeast Asia that modernization has promoted modern marital behavior at the expense of the traditional marriage institution (Heaton et al., 2001; Hirschman and Teerawichitchainan, 2003; Jones, 1994; Leete, 1994).

Model 1 of Table 2 also shows that the logistic regression coefficient for *Gender* is not statistically significant, suggesting that the odds of love marriages are evenly distributed among men and women in Kuala Lumpur. Additionally, Model 1 shows that education is negatively associated with parental arrangement: the lower the educational level one has achieved, the less likely he or she reports a love marriage. This finding is consistent with those reported in the existing studies of marriage patterns in Islamic Southeast Asia that education is a key determinant of modern marital behavior for both the Malays and the Chinese (Heaton et al., 2001; Hirschman and Teerawichitchainan, 2003; Jones, 1994; Leete, 1994). Finally, Model 1 of Table 2 shows that *Malay ethnicity* is positively related to the dependent variable and the relationship is statistically significant.

Model 2 of Table 2 uses both social status variables and family background variables. The overall patterns of the effects of education, gender, and birth cohorts in this model are similar to those reported in Model 1 of Table 2. This model also shows that traditional family background has a negative effect on free

Table 2
Multivariate Analysis of Predictors of Free Choice, Kuala Lumpur

Covariates	*Model 1*	*Model 2*
Age cohort		
Before 1950	-.824 (.143)*	-.814 (.144)*
1950-1959	-.384 (.131)*	-.366 (.132)*
1960-1969	-.217 (.134)	-.209 (.135)
Gender	-.022 (.101)	-.051 (.102)
Education		
Below primary school	-2.115 (.299)*	-1.715 (.318)*
Primary school	-1.516 (.179)*	-1.220 (.197)*
Junior high school	-.882 (.170)*	-.691 (.180)*
Senior high school	-.523 (.160)*	-.414 (.164)*
Vocational school	-.453 (.314)	-.422 (.315)
Work	.115 (.113)	.118 (.115)
Rural father	—	-.358 (.129)*
Father education		
Below primary school	—	-.512 (.202)*
Primary school	—	-.325 (.182)
Junior high school	—	-.368 (.210)
Malay ethnicity	-.259 (.100)*	-.224 (.104)*
2-log likelihood	2,421.589	2,402.287
df	11	15
N	1,967	1,967

Note: Numbers in parentheses are standard errors. *p < .05. The reference group for Age cohort is the respondents who were born after 1970; for Education, university & above; and for Father education, senior high school.

choice: the respondents are less likely to report a free choice marriage if their fathers had a low level of education or were rural farmers when they got married. Finally, Model 2 shows that controlling status attainment and family background does not remove the Malay-Chinese difference in free choice. The Malays are subject to more parental control than the Chinese. This finding is consistent with those reported in existing research that significant ethnic variations in marriage persist even with key variables controlled in multivariate analysis (Brien and Lillard, 1994: 1, 185-6; Hirschman and Teerawichitchainan, 2003: 244; also see Anderson et al., 1987; Heaton et al., 2001; Jones, 1994; Leete, 1996).

Next, to examine the above-mentioned gendered explanation of inter-group variation in free choice, four logistic regression analyses are performed on the women sub-sample and the men sub-sample respectively. It can be seen that the general patterns regarding education reported in Table 2 repeat themselves in Table 3. Education apparently has similar effects on both women and men with regard to their preference for free choice. However, there is a reverse trend in free choice among women in Kuala Lumpur as the third birth cohort reports greater odds of arranged marriages than the second birth cohort, which is consistent with the news reports that arranged marriage has made a comeback in Malaysia recently (Mahmood, 2003). No similar patterns are found among men, nevertheless.

Equally important, Table 3 shows different effects of *Worker*, *Rural father*, and *Father education* on women and men with regard to free choice. Working women are more likely than non-working women to experience romances, women with a rural father are less likely than women with an urban father to rely on free choice to find a prospective mate, and women with well-educated fathers are less likely to be influenced by their parents than women with poorly-educated fathers. No similar patterns are found among men, however. These findings suggest that low status (and hence more traditional) parents have more control over their daughters than over their sons, which in turn explains the greater impact of work on women's probabilities for free choice than on men's.

Finally, Models 1 and 2 of Table 3 show that controlling for status attainment and family background variables, Malay women are significantly less likely than Chinese women to

Table 3
Multivariate Analysis of Predictors of Free Choice by Gender

Covariates	*Women*		*Men*	
	Model 1	*Model 2*	*Model 3*	*Model 4*
Age cohort				
Before 1950	-.470 (.220)*	-.511 (.223)*	-.994 (.193)*	-.969 (.194)*
1950-1959	-.229 (.189)	-.194 (.192)	-.436 (.184)*	-.424 (.186)*
1960-1969	-.411 (.175)*	-.410 (.178)*	.165 (.219)	-.175 (.220)
Education				
Below primary school	-2.096 (.394)*	-1.645 (.421)*	-2.335 (.510)*	-2.029 (.535)*
Primary school	-1.629 (.272)*	-1.275 (.295)*	-1.431 (.246)*	-1.241 (.275)*
Junior high school	-.887 (.259)*	-.611 (.272)*	-.881 (.230)*	-.803 (.247)*
Senior high school	-.603 (.245)*	-.465 (.250)	-.446 (.215)*	-.397 (.224)
Vocational school	-.272 (.567)	-.267 (.569)	-.600 (.384)	-.546 (.388)
Worker	.480 (.152)*	.470 (.154)*	.293 (.178)	-.301 (.179)
Rural father	—	-.451 (.186)*	—	-.254 (.183)
Father education				
Below primary school	—	-.644 (.279)*	—	-.281 (.299)
Primary school	—	-.581 (.250)*	—	.002 (.272)
Junior high school	—	-.466 (.289)	—	-.257 (.312)
Malay ethnicity	-.409 (.141)*	-.377 (.148)*	-.064 (.146)	-.032 (.150)
2-log likelihood	1.233.378	1,217.244	1,161.227	1,151.091
df	10	14	10	14
N	1,000	1,000	967	967

Note: Numbers in parentheses are standard errors. *p < .05.
The reference group for Age cohort is the respondents who were born after 1970; for Education, university & above; and for Father education, senior high schoo.

describe their marriages as love unions. In comparison, there is no similar inter-group difference in free choice between Malay men and Chinese men. This finding is consistent with the above discussion on the effect of gender on parental control in the post-1990 marriage market in Malaysia. It also suggests that the gender difference may be responsible for the ethnic variation in free choice. This suggestion may contribute to a better understanding of the effect of Malay culture and status attainment on ethnic variation in marriage in urban Malaysia.

SUMMARY AND DISCUSSIONS

As noted, existing studies show significant Malay-Chinese differences in love marriage in the pre-1990 era and explain them in terms of Malay culture and ethnic disparity in social status. The data sets used in these studies, e.g. the Malaysian

Marriage Survey and the Malaysian Population and Family Survey, were collected before or in 1988. There may have been significant changes in marriage in Malaysia since then, given the diminishing impact of Malay culture on marriage and reduced ethnic disparity in social status. Is there still a Malay-Chinese variation in free choice? If the answer is yes, how can it be explained?

To answer these questions, a mass survey was conducted in Kuala Lumpur in 2002 to collect retrospective marital histories. Consistent with the existing studies of marital behavior in pre-1990 Malaysia, this research shows increasing probabilities of love matches among both the Malays and the Chinese. Also consistent with the existing studies, this research finds a greater preference for free choice among the Chinese than that among the Malays in multivariate analyses. This research also uses gender to understand how Malay culture and status attainment affect inter-group differences in marriage. In other words, it does not just use Malay culture and status attainment to explain Malay-Chinese differences in love marriage. More importantly, it studies how gender mediates the effects of these two variables on ethnic variation in free choice in Malaysia. It is possible that culture and status attainment affect Malay women and Malay men differently. Indeed, this research finds that controlling family background and status attainment removes inter-group differences in free choice between Malay men and Chinese men but not those between Malay women and Chinese women. This gender difference may be responsible for Malay-Chinese differences in love marriage in urban Malaysia.

There is room for improvement, however. For example, only 30 percent of the sampled respondents participated in the 2002 Kuala Lumpur Survey. Although this is a fairly common problem that every researcher faces when doing survey research in major cities in Malaysia, it does suggest that findings from this research should be interpreted with caution. Field observations suggest that the findings reported in this research may represent mainly the marriage patterns of middle and low status residents in the city. Further research is needed to study higher status residents in guarded residences. Also, the respondents were sampled from the population aged between 18 and 65. Older and younger residents were not included in the survey. Nor are divorced and widowed respondents included in the survey. The marital histories of these people, if included in the sample, may alter the results of data analysis in this research. Finally, it is important to emphasize that the findings from this research are based on survey data from Kuala Lumpur. A nationally selected sample may present a different picture.

Despite these potential and real shortcomings, by comparing the Malays and the Chinese who do not differ greatly in education and occupational attainment, this research shows some recent changes in mate selection and the effect of status attainment and Malay culture on inter-group differences in marital behavior in urban Malaysia. More importantly, this research shows how gender mediates the effects of status attainment and Malay culture on inter-group differences in marriage in the post-1990 era. Further research is recommended to confirm this gendered explanation with a more representative sample from Malaysia.

NOTES

I would like to thank the reviewers of International Journal of Sociology of the Family for helpful comments on an earlier version of this paper. I also thank Kevin Hewison, Alex Kwan, and Vivienne Wee for their assistance in preparing the 2001 Survey and my field research in Kuala Lumpur. Funding support for this research is from a grant from Southeast Asia Research Centre at the City University of Hong Kong and a Strategic Research Grant from the City University of Hong Kong (Project # 7001377). Southeast Asia Research Centre supported my field research in Kuala Lumpur in December 2002.

1. A reviewer of *International Journal of Sociology of the Family* mentions that Malays were 50% of the total population, or 53% of Malaysian citizens. If one deals with Peninsular Malaysia, Malays were 58.7% of the population.
2. The third largest ethnic group is Indians, who represents nearly 8 percent of the population in Malaysia. Consistent with the main research interests of the existing studies of Islamic Southeast Asia, I focus on Malay-Chinese differences in marriage in this paper. Hopefully a comparative study of the three main ethnic groups can be conducted if resources become available in the future.
3. Other dimensions of experiences and subjectivities can also be productively used to understand how they interact with Malay culture and status attainment to influence marriage patterns. This task however is beyond the scope of this research.
4. I thank a reviewer of *International Journal of Sociology of the Family* for corrections on marriages between a Muslim groom and a non-Muslim bride.

5. For information on this metropolitan area, see Bunnell (2004).
6. I thank a reviewer of *International Journal of Sociology of the Family* for his or her view on this issue.
7. Some scholars suggest that I use marriage cohorts instead. I find similar results when using marriage cohorts or birth cohorts in data analysis.
8. These findings do not suggest that the Chinese are behind the Malays in all aspects of status attainment. In fact, I find that their family income levels are higher than those of the Malays. A plausible explanation is Chinese entrepreneurial activities and their concentration in commerce in Kuala Lumpur. These occupations do not require a great deal of education yet may yield higher earnings than jobs in the civil services and the formal school system where the Malays are concentrated.

REFERENCES

Andaya, Barbara Watson and Andaya, Leonard Y. (2001), A History of Malaysia. Honolulu: University of Hawaii Press.

Anderson, Kathryn H., Hill, M. Anne, and Butler, J. S. (1987), Age at Marriage in Malaysia. *Journal of Development Economics,* 26, 2: 223-234.

Blackburn, Robert, Jennifer Jarman, and Bradley Brooks. (2000), The Puzzle of Gender Segregation and Inequality: A Cross-National Analysis. European Sociological Review, 16, 2: 119-35.

Brien, Michael J. and Lillard, Lee A. (1994), Education, Marriage, and First Conception in Malaysia. The Journal of Human Resources, 29, 4: 1167-1204.

Bunnell, Tim. (2004), Malaysia, Modernity, and the Multimedia Super Corridor. London: RoutledgeCurzon.

Caldwell, John C. (1996), Forward. In Richard Leete, Malaysia's Demographic Transition (pp. vii-ix). Kuala Lumpur: Oxford University Press.

Carolan, Marsha T. (1999), Contemporary Muslim Women and the Family. in Harriette Pipes McAdoo, (Ed.) Family Ethnicity (pp. 213-21). Thousand Oaks: Sage Publications.

Gillette, Maris Boyd. (2000), Between Mecca and Beijing. Stanford: Stanford University Press.

Goode, William J. (1963), World Revolution and Family Patterns. New York: The Free Press.

Haddad, Yvonne Yazbeck (1991), The Muslims of America. New York: Oxford University Press.

Hamayotsu, Kikue (2002), Islam and Nation Building in Southeast Asia: Malaysia and Indonesia in Comparative Perspective. Pacific Affairs, 75, 3: 353–375.

Heaton, Tim B. (1996), Socioeconomic and Familial Status of Women Associated with Age at First Marriage in Three Islamic Societies. *Journal of Comparative Family Studies,* 27, 1: 41-59.

Heaton, Tim B., Cammacj, Mark, and Young, Larry. (2001), Why Is the Divorce Rate Declining in Indonesia? *Journal of Marriage and the Family,* 63, 2: 480-490.

Hirschman, Charles and Teerawichitchainan, Bussarawan. (2003), Cultural and Socioeconomic Influences on Divorce during Modernization: Southeast Asia, 1940s to 1960s. Population and Development Review, 29, 2: 215-253.

Holland, Lorien. (2001), A Lesson in Race Relations. Far Eastern Economic Review, (7 June), 164, 22: 28-29.

Inkeles, Alex. (1969), Making Men Modern. *American Journal of Sociology,* 75, 2: 208-225.

Jones, Gavin W. (1981), Malay Marriage and Divorce in Peninsular Malaysia: Three Decades of Change. Population and Development Review, 7, 2: 255-78.

——. (1994), Marriage and Divorce in Islamic Southeast Asia. Kuala Lumpur: Oxford University Press.

——. (1997), Modernization and Divorce: Contrasting Trends in Islamic Southeast Asia and the West. Population and Development Review, 23, 1: 95-114.

Kheng, Cheah Boon. (2002), Malaysia: The Making of a Nation Singapore: Institute of Southeast Asian Studies.

Koon, Heng Pek. (1997), The New Economic Policy and the Chinese Community in Peninsular Malaysia. Developing Economics, 35, 3: 262-292.

Leete, Richard. (1994). The Continuing Flight from Marriage and Parenthood among the Overseas Chinese in East and Southeast Asia: Dimensions and Implication. Population and Development Review, 20, 4: 811-829.

——. (1996), Malaysia's Demographic Transition. Kuala Lumpur: Oxford University Press.

Mabry, T. J. (1998). Modernization, Nationalism and Islam. Ethnic and Racial Studies, 21, 1: 64-88.

Mahmood, Kazi (2003), Arranged Marriages Still Popular in Malaysia. Kuala Lumpur, IslamOnline.net: Thursday, December 25.

Martinez, Patricia A. (2001), The Islamic State or the State of Islam in Malaysia. Contemporary Southeast Asia, 23, 3: 474–503.

Morgan, S. Phillip, Stash, Sharon, Herbert, Smith, and Mason, Karen Oppenheim. (2002), Muslim and Non-Muslim Differences in Female Autonomy and Fertility. Population and Development Review, 28, 3: 515-538.

Pimentel, Ellen Efron. (2000), Just How Do I Love Thee?: Marital Relations in Urban China. *Journal of Marriage and the Family,* 62, 1: 32-48.

Raslan, Karim. (1996), Malaysia in Transition. Singapore: Times Books International.

Rindfuss, Ronald R., Minja Kim Choe, Larry L Bumpass, Noriko O Tsuya (2004), Social Networks and Family Change in Japan. American Sociological Review, 69, 6: 838-861.

Seguino, Stephanie. (2000a), Accounting for Gender in Asian Economic Growth. Feminist Economics, 6, 3: 27-58.

——. (2000b), Gender Inequality and Economic Growth: A Cross-Country Analysis. World Development, 28, 7: 1211-1230.

Selvaratnam, V. (1988), Ethnicity, Inequality and Higher Education in Malaysia. Comparative Education Review, 32, 2: 173-196.

Sherif, Bahira. (1999), Islamic Family Ideals and Their Relevance to American Muslim Families. In Harriette Pipes McAdoo, (Ed.) Family Ethnicity (pp. 203-12). Thousand Oaks: Sage Publications.

Strange, Heather. (1976), Continuity and Change. *Journal of Marriage and the Family,* 38, 3: 561-571.

Sudha, S. (1997). Family Size, Sex Composition and Children's Education: Ethnic Differentials over Development in Peninsular Malaysia. Population Studies, 51, 2: 139-151.

Tan, Poo Chang and Gavin W. Jones. (1990), Changing Patterns of Marriage and Household Formation in Peninsular Malaysia. Sojourn, 5, 2: 163-193.

Yeung, Henry Wai-chung. (2000), Economic Globalization, Crisis and the Emergence of Chinese Business Communities in Southeast Asia. International Sociology, 15, 2: 266-287.

4

WHO TAKES CARE OF THEIR CHILDREN WHEN MOTHERS WORK: A CASE STUDY OF CHINESE URBAN WORKING MOTHERS

Sue Ya Xu

INTRODUCTION

At least since 1950s, the urban female employment rate in China is among the highest in the world (Croll, 1983, 1994, 1995; Adams & Winston, 1980; Andors, 1983:30-32 and 80-89; ILO, 2000; World Bank, 2005). By the 1970s, there were only about 10 percent of urban women not employed full-time in the waged labor force and they were mainly the elderly and retired, the weak, the disabled and those who were awaiting job assignment" (Croll, 1983:43).

A detailed survey on urban households in five cities of China confirms a continuation of the situation through the 1980s as well as the 1990s. In the 1980s, most working aged urban women, regardless marital statuses, were employed (Project of Household Research of Five Cities, 1985:18). More than 90 percent of urban families in the 1990s were dual-earner households (Institute of Population Studies, 1994:39). Recent statistics shows that the high female labor force participation rate has continued into the twenty first century (World Bank, 2005).

One of the longstanding special features of the high female employment in urban China is the large proportion of working mothers working on a full-time basis. There are at least two reasons for it. Firstly, till the 1990s, Chinese women had a comparatively high marriage rate and a comparatively low voluntary childlessness. And they took marriage and a stable family as the essential components and purpose of life (Zha, 1991:500; Zeng,1995), despite the process of modernization in both the economic and social realms. Census data of 1982 and

1990 show that the percentage of urban women never married was less than 4 percent by age 30 and less than 1 percent by age 34 (Zeng, 1991a: 25, 1991b; Jiang, 1995; Zha, 1991). Most of the couples preferred to have at least one child and 87.7 percent of the wives in 1990 had completed their first birth before age 30 (Zeng, 1991b: table 9).

Secondly, flexible working hours, as a measure of family friendly employment, has not yet been initiated in China. For urban residents, part-time jobs and casual working hours have been a recent phenomenon after the rise of unemployment and layoffs in the late 1990s. These jobless, once unable to (re-)engage full time employment, often have to take casual works or become self-employed though this does not affect the rate of urban labor force participation statistically. Since the labor force participation rate is calculated as the proportion of the working age groups of the population in concern that is economically active, anyone engaged in any way in the production of goods and services during a specified period, full-time or part-time, is classified as economically active. However, their number should not exceed 10 percent of the total labor force according to the estimation of the size of the unemployment rate and the layoffs (Won, 2004; Tang, 2004:15; Gu, 2003; Tan & Li, 2005).

Between the 1970s-1990s, more than one third of the urban labor force in China was composed of working mothers in full-time employment. Given the inherent incompatibility between childcare and mothers' working careers, these mothers needed external resources to solve the role-conflict. Who was the "helping hand" looking after the child when the mother was at work? This question has always concerned policy-makers as well as scholars. To this end, the paper will examine childcare arrangements made by working mothers in these three decades.

COMMERCIALIZATION: THE CHANGE IN CHILDCARE PROVISIONS

The profound socio-economic changes in the past half century in China have altered the faces of childcare providers in the cities. The planned system established in the 1950s introduced women into full-time employment, and the family-based individual-centered childcare tradition was then replaced by an outside-the-home and collective-centered childcare system (Onesto, 1998). Before the Socialist Revolution of 1949 in China, the functional importance of a woman laid in her reproductive role; ideally producing male descendants for a patriarchal family. A strict sexual division of labor assured that she undertook total responsibility for childcare and other household functions. In practice, however, other women from the father's family, especially the paternal grandmother, often shared the responsibility of looking after the child especially if it was a male. After the revolution, with the campaign of gender equality, the male preference culture was criticized and in the cities; many girls were looked after by their paternal and maternal grandmothers who were involved in childcare. Although men began to contribute more than ever to housework, it was still not widely accepted for men to take a major role in childcare. To enable women to more fully participate in building a new socialist society, the central government created a welfare system in which the childcare service was an integrated part of the development program. It was sanctioned by the government but in most cases the work units (*Danwei*), like the SOEs, were responsible for its implementation. Most of the SOEs have since then on established childcare facilities such as childcare centers, kindergartens, and nursery rooms in accordance to the standard of requirement of the government. The government's services were only directed to those who were outside the labor force, and not a significant population. Official figures indicate that in 1988 more than 93 percent of the kindergartens in China were run by the work units (All-China Women's Union & Shaan-xi Women's Union, 1991:121). Employees of the work units were entitled to use these services with subsidized prices. In 1951 there were less than 5000 kindergartens in the country, with an enrollment of less than 400,000; by 1978 the number reached 164,000 with nearly 8 million children. The number of kindergarten increased to more than 170,000 in 1988 (All-China Women's Union & Shaan-xi Women's Union, 1991:121) and over 187,000 in 1996 (*China Statistical Yearbook 1999*). The size of the enrollment expanded to 18.5 million in 1988 (All-China Women's Union & *Shaan-xi* Women's Union, 1991:121) and to 26.7 million in 1996 (*China Statistical Yearbook 1999*). Such a work unit based childcare services made outside home care accessible to working women (Adams and Winston, 1980:15-16; Onesto, 1998) and therefore made it possible for them to keep their jobs after becoming mothers.

However, the work unit based childcare system has faced severe challenges after the start of the economic reforms in 1978. In the reform era, SOEs have had to increasingly respond to market rather than the state. The reform has pushed SOEs to earn an increasing proportion of their budget in the market. During the 1980s competition forced many SOEs, even the profit-making ones, to reduce their welfare expenditure. In 1997, SOEs in China were in a tripartite situation with approximately one third earning a profit, one third breaking even, and another one third in the red. Among the SOEs with financial difficulties, childcare services were noted to be severely under-funded. Some childcare services, which used to be free of charge or heavily subsidized, have been partly or totally "marketized"; others simply had to shut down. As a result, the number of kindergartens has been steadily declining since the mid-1990s, and by 2001 there were less than 112,000 kindergartens operating in the country (*China Statistical Yearbook 2002*) compared to 187,000 in 1996.

On the other hand, the introduction of the market mechanism has brought in more channels for childcare provisions. Since the early 1980s, an increasing number of rural girls have migrated to urban areas to work as *Bao mu* (Tan & Li, 2005; Mertes, 2002),—doing household chores and taking care of the old or young. *Bao mu* existed before the economic reforms. As a matter of fact, apart from the family care, *Bao mu* was the only childcare service outside the planned system. Such a private provision persisted during strict state control primarily because it often appeared as a part of domestic matters. At that time, a *Bao mu* found her job mainly through family connections—she was either the family's distant relative living in the countryside or an acquaintance of the family's rural relative, who happened to have time to help. Therefore, a *Bao mu* was more like a kind of support from the extended family; there was no contract between a *Bao mu* and the family she served. No matter how the mother needed her, when the work on the farm became busy and her own family called her back, or she was discovered by the local police for illegally residing in the city, she would have to return to the countryside. Her accommodation was covered by her host any the salary for the *Bao mu*'s service varied. Indeed it was not unusual that the reward for her service would be just some "gifts"—such as a set of new dress, some presents to her family, etc. At the same time, being a *Bao mu* provided a chance, the only chance perhaps, for a rural girl to experience the city life under the strict rural-urban migration control. Since the economic reforms, and following the relaxation of rural-urban migration control, *Bao mu*, now equivalent to nannies or au pairs, has become the rural women's established profession in the cities. Though some of the *Bao mu* still find jobs through personal connections, they are increasingly introduced to the urban families by domestic service companies, with clearly defined services specifications and standard pay rates according to the skills and the responsibilities. Many enterprising businessmen and women have established private nurseries, kindergartens, and pre-school education centers under reform policies permitting private enterprise (Robert 1994). They, together with other market facilities, have provided the commercial childcare. However, they are often expensive and there have been reports on the problems of regulating and monitoring the services.

RESEARCH PURPOSE AND DESIGN

While the decline of the work unit based welfare system and the rise of commercial childcare service has been widely observed (Mertes, 2002; Tan and Li, 2005), accurate longitudinal quantitative descriptions on the impacts of such changes on working mothers' childcare arrangements have been rare. This paper helps fill the niche. A case study on 260 working mothers in two SOEs in Beijing was carried out. Besides collecting the general information, the questionnaires were distributed to record age-and cohort-specific information on childcare arrangement for each child. The data are sufficient for the construction of a Multi-state Childcare Status Life Table. A distinct advantage of Life-table analysis is that it enables us to use cross-sectional data to trace longitudinal dynamics (Eltigani, 2000; 2001). That is to say, with Multi-state Childcare Status Life Table we are able to describe the changes on working mothers' childcare arrangements over the periods from 1970s to 1990s.

Before discussing the data collection and model building, below is a description of the two SOEs and the childcare provisions provided to their employees.

The Two SOEs: B1 and B2

Two SOEs in Beijing were chosen based on the consideration that they were typical sate enterprises and together could provide an ideal case to observe the changes of childcare arrangements by ordinary urban Chinese female workers. For confidentiality reasons, the two SOEs will simply be referred to here as B1 and B2, which happen to be two large wool spinning-weaving enterprises under the jurisdiction of the Textile Bureau of the Municipality of Beijing. By July 1997, B1 had 2571 employees and B2 had 2827. Women accounted for 70 percent of the total employees and thus childcare had always been an important welfare program in both of the SOEs.

The two SOEs were originally one enterprise before they split into two in 1985. Before the economic reforms started in 1978, like all other SOEs, the government determined the production as well as the usage of the profits, while the state was also responsible for all the costs and losses. After the economic reforms, however, the relationship between the state and the SOEs changed. During the 1990s the state, gradually handed over the responsibilities of production, profit distribution, and management to the enterprises. The direct investment was replaced by loans, as these and other changes were made to stimulate productivity and to turn the SOEs into independent economic entities. The new freedom and the new market had brought about a rise in production in the 1980s. As a result, the two previous sub-factories–one specializing in thin fabric for the spring and autumn cloth market and the other focusing on thicker wool materials-expanded into two independent enterprises in 1985. The former is here labeled B1 and the later B2. Since then the two SOEs have experienced different business fortunes.

Because of higher investment in technology and better management, and despite some ups-and-downs, by the time of our survey, B1 had been successful in profit-making. By the end of 1996, it recorded a net profit of more than 12 million yuan. B2, on the other hand, after several years of being prosperous, has run into losses since the early 1990s. Besides the mistakes made by management and low investment in technology innovation, the shrinkage of its product market due to the rise of new winter cloth materials and the severe competition from the non-state enterprises had played a vital role in its financial problems. By the end of 1996, B2 recorded a loss of 12 million yuan. Before they split, workers of both of the SOEs had their salaries pegged to the same pay scale, but after the split a discernible income gap appeared and grew between the two SOEs, and by 1997, the workers of B2 on average earned 33 percent less than their counterparts in B1.

Both SOEs provided an-hour-a-day free breast-feeding time for the female employees, and they also had a policy not to assign female workers with young children to the night-shift. Both SOEs shared a non-profit *You er yuan* (combination of nursery and kindergarten) built before they split, which accepted children of age 3 month to 6 years. The *You er yuan* provided childcare for up to 10 hours on every working day and used to only serve the employees of B1 and B2 before it opened to the public in 1990. But till 1998, children of B1 and B2 could enjoy a subsidized price (120 yuan a month) whilst non-employees had to pay a market rate of 200 yuan a month for the same service.

Although the employees paid less than the market rate for the service of the *You er yuan*, judging from the ratio of the service price to the average wage, the service had become increasingly expensive. In the 1970s, the charge for childcare in the *You er yuan* was about 3 yuan per child per month and the average wage of workers was about 35 yuan; the ratio of childcare cost over the average wage was 0.086. In the mid 1980s, without any fundamental improvement in service, the cost of childcare for employees increased to about 15 yuan per month whereas the wage increased to about 120 yuan. The ratio increased to 0.125. By July 1997 the cost of childcare was 120 yuan. This means that for the employees of B1, whose average wage was 894 yuan (std. deviation=219 yuan), the ratio was 0.134; and for the employees of B2, whose average wage was 598 yuan (std. deviation = 128 yuan), the ratio became 0.201. The increase in the ratio of the *You er yuan* fee to the average wage reflects the significant reduction of welfare support for childcare from the work units. And for the employees in B2, childcare cost them as much as 20 percent of their wages.

In brief, the women in the B1 and B2 shared the same standard of living while together and yet each has carried out a different "life" after leaving the "parents' home." Such a special connection between the two SOEs enables us to observe the impacts of the economic transition on the working mothers' childcare arrangements.

DATA COLLECTION AND METHOD

Data Collection. Have working mothers from B1 and B2 reacted differently in different socio-economic circumstances? How has the change in the relative costs of childcare after the reforms reshaped the working mothers' childcare arrangements? With these questions in mind, from May 1997 to May 1998, we carried out a sample survey in B1 and B2 respectively. The reference time was 1 July 1997.

The target group was fulltime working mothers. After a pilot survey, a simple stratified sampling was applied to 10 percent of the target group. This method requires us to classify the target population into a number of blocks according to certain criteria and then, to select a random sample from each block. We used this method based on two considerations. First, theoretically this method can reduce random errors more than the simple random sampling and thus provides a better representative value to the whole. Second, from a practical perspective, this method is handy to use as each SOE naturally stratifies their employees in different working departments.

As shown in Table 1, 129 female employees were selected from B1, of which, 122 were the mothers of a single child and 7 were mothers of two. Their mean age by July 1997 was 38.1 (std. deviation = 6). In B2 the number surveyed was 131, 125 of them had one child at the time of survey and 6 had two children. Their mean age was 37.6 (std. deviation=6). The small number of women with two children reflects the effective family planning programs in the cities. Before 1980, the policy was "later marriage, longer birth interval and fewer children (*Wan xi shao*)", which promoted no more than two children per couple. This policy had significantly reduced the average number of children per household in the big cities of China like Beijing. Since 1980, a "one-child" policy has been effectively implemented. No women in our database have more than two children. In our sample, 247 women, accounting for 95 percent of the total, have only one child, while 13 women are mothers of two children.

Every working mother was required to specify, for each of her children, the person or agent who was the prime childcare provider when she was at work. In the end, an age-cohort-and SOE- specific database on care providers was established for a total of 273 children, of which, the mothers of 136 were from B1 and 137 were from B2 (Table 1).

Table 1
Working Mothers and Their Children by Birth Cohort
(Results of the Sample Survey)

Mothers' affiliation and parity of children		*Number working mother*	*Number of Children by birth cohort* 1970s	1980s	1990s	sub total
B1	1st child		17	89	23	129
	2nd child		4	3	0	7
	sub total	129	21	92	23	136
B2	1st child		20	86	25	131
	2nd child		6	0	0	6
	sub total	131	26	86	25	137
Total		260	47	178	48	273

Source: survey in B1 and B2, May 1997 to May 1998.

Retrospective records represent the most suitable sources for our study. However, recall errors such as omission or inaccurate timing of the event are a common feature of this type of data. Since the propensity to forget is stronger for the events that occurred in the more distant past, the information provided for the children born in the 1970s may contain higher inaccuracies than that for those born in the later decades. However, given the small number of births each of the working mothers experienced (no more than two), which certainly helps to reduce the recall bias, the quality of the data is considered reliable for such in-depth and quantitative research.

Method. As mentioned previously, family members, the welfare system, and commercial services have been the main "agents" providing childcare services in China in the past fifty years. How have these three "agents" served working mothers in the 1970s, 1980s, and 1990s?

To answer the question we need to estimate the children of each cohort the probabilities of the transition between the care statuses. Life table analysis is the most appropriate method to do the task not only because it is ideal for studying mobility or transitions between life statues (Schoen 1988; Willekens et al. 1982), but also because it offers a solution to the problem of censoring that is commonly encountered when life-events utilize cross-sectional data (2000: 1; 2002: 4). Its application has reached far beyond demographic studies and into studies on labor market, migration, and marital changes (Willekens et al., 1982; Schoen, 1975, 1988; Rogers, 1973a, 1973b, 1975; Schoen and Nelson,

1974; Rogers and Ledent, 1975, 1976; Ledent, 1980; Zeng 1991a, 1993, Xu, 2000).

With respect to establishing a Multistate Childcare Status Life Table, three categories of the care statuses are identified. We denote them by "f", "w", and "c" respectively. Here, "f" means that family members including grandparents and other female relatives may take the responsibility of childcare when the mother is at work. The father is not considered in this category which reflects the traditional sexual division of labor and women's role as care provider. This traditional women's role still has deep roots in Chinese culture and influences married couples' lives (Xu A. 2005, Xie H. 1990). With the consideration that childcare as well as other chores is still not regarded as husbands' duty, we do not include the father as a care taker in our model. The second category "w" refers to the situation in which a child is looked after by welfare facilities like the *You er yuan* in the SOEs; and "c" applies to the situation in which a child receives care from a private commercial care provider such as a *Bao mu*, or a private childcare centre etc. (see Table 2).

Table 2
Three Child Care Statuses

Status	*Definition*
f	Child is under the care of a family member such as grandparents or other
w	female relatives;
c	Child is under the care of a welfare facility, such as the *You er yuan* provided by the SOEs; Child is under the care of commercial care agent, like *Bao mu* or private kindergarten, etc.

During a mother's maternity leave, is assumed to be the prime care taker for her child even though she may do so with help from a supporting caretaker. However, after she resumes her full time work, she must find someone else to replace her as the child's prime caretaker. That is to say, when the childcare arrangement begins depends on the mother's length of maternity leave. Before the economic reforms, the length of maternity leave was 56 days with full pay; after the reform, a female worker could extend her maternity leave to a maximum for half a year at reduced pay (usually at 70 percent of her wage) during her extended leave. Since the 1990s, the time of official paid maternity leave has extended to 90 days. Before the labor reconstruction between 1993 to 1998, some SOEs with a surplus labor force allowed their female employees to take maternity leave for as long as 180 days or even longer, with compensation being further reduced even to zero. However, the majority of female employees in all circumstances returned to work within a year. Therefore, typically the one year old age mark is set to be the starting point of our observation. Children in China start their primary schools at age 6 or 7, so we assumed that after a child reaches age 6, (s)he will no longer needs the care like a pre-school child does. The age interval of our observation is thus from age 1 to age 6.

The work of the Multistate Childcare Life Table is represented graphically in Figure 1. The initial state is the child under "the care of her/his mother" before age 1, and from there a transition begins into and between three other possible care statuses, either under the care of family member 'f', a welfare facility 'w' or commercial service 'c'.

The three care statuses, "f", "w", "c", are transient events within the age interval under observation. For instance, a boy might be first cared for by a *Bao mu* at age 1 after the initial

Figure 1

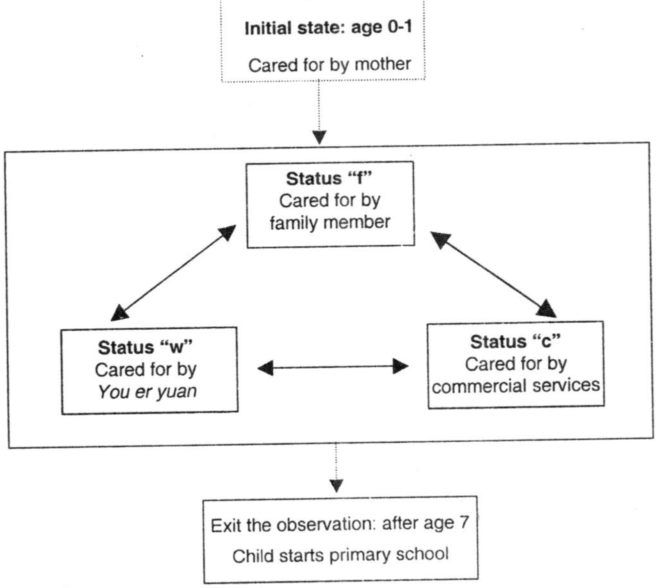

state (age 0-1, cared for by his mother). After a year the *Bao mu* leaves and his mother sends him to a nursery run by her work unit; a year later his mother finds another *Bao mu* and he then returns to status "c". When he reaches age 4 his mother puts him to kindergarten again and this changes his status again to "w" where he stays till he starts primary school. We can say that this boy experienced 4 states of transition between 2 statuses–"c" and "w" during his time between 1 to 6 years of age.

The following is the brief description of the mathematic expression of the construction of the Multistate Childcare Life Table. The details can be found in the works of Willekens at al. (1982) and Zeng (1991a).

First, the instantaneous rate, $R_{ij,}$ of transition from status i to j for a child at the age x is computed:

$$R_{ij}(x)=\begin{bmatrix} R_{ff}(x) & R_{fw}(x) & R_{fc}(x) \\ R_{wf}(x) & R_{ww}(x) & R_{wc}(x) \\ R_{cf}(x) & R_{cw}(x) & R_{cc}(x) \end{bmatrix}$$

Second, from these rates, a set of transition probabilities, P_{ij}, can be derived from

$$P_{ij}(x)=[1+0.5nR_{ij}(x)]^{-1}[1-0.5nR_{ij}(x)]$$

where i, j represents the childcare status "f", "w", or "c" and 'n' is the age interval. In this study, for the age 1 to 3 we use a single-year age interval and for 4-6 we use an age interval of 3 years. Such a choice is a result of technical constraint. As limited by the length of questionnaire, it is hard to record the childcare situation for every single age. We thus have to give priority to the younger ages (i.e. the age 1-3) when the need for childcare is more pressing.

Third, we calculate the number of children who shifted the care status from "j" at the age x to that of "i" at age x+n:

$$_{jx}l_i(x+n)=\sum_{k=1}^{n} p_{ki}(x)l_k(x)$$

Where n is the number of states (in this case, 3)

The total number of children at age x+n can be presented in the following form:

$$l(x+n) = P(x)\, l(x)$$

After the life-table population was calculated, it was straightforward to derive the sojourn time in each state:

$$Li(x) = {}^{n}/_{2}\,[l_i(x) + l_i(x+n)]$$

According to our assumption that no childcare service is needed when the child reaches the age 7; thus, L(7) = 0. The number of child-years with status 'i' living beyond the age x is computed by:

$$T_i(x) = \sum_{t=x}^{6} [L_i(t)] \qquad (1 \leq t \leq 6)$$

Finally, the expected year a child under the care of 'i' during the period from age 1 to age 6 is counted by:

$$e_i = T_i(1)/l_i(1)$$

FINDINGS

Childcare arrangements over the decades–the result of the cohort comparisons

The result of the life table analysis demonstrates that, in the three decades from the 1970s to the 1990s, the *You er yuan* provided the longest childcare services for children aged 1-6 of the working mothers of B1 or B2. This was followed by family-based care, which covered on average 30-40 percent of the total care time needed, and the amount of the care provided by the family members had been increasing significantly after the reforms. Commercial services provided no more than 5 percent of the total care needed. The women of B1 with children born in the 1990s, whose average wage was higher, used commercial services for their children 2.5 times more often than their counterparts in B2. The details of the care time each "agent" provided to the working mothers are given in column 1 in Table 3. During the first 6 years of care, a working mother's care arrangement would be as follow: If her child was born in the 1970s, the mother would let family member(s) look after her/him for about 21 months and would put her/him in the *You er yuan* for nearly 4 years. The commercial service would only help for about 3 months during the 6 year period. If her child was born in the 1980s, before (s)he reached age 7, the duration spent in the care of family member(s) would increase slightly to more than 2 years, and the *You er yuan* would look after her/him for around 3 years and 10 months. The au pair, nanny or private kindergarten care would decline to about 2.5 months. If the child was born in the 1990s, the time spent under the care of the family member(s) is expected to be extended to 2.5 years whereas the time spent in the *You er yuan* would be further reduced to 37 months, a reduction of 11 months and 9 months compared to the cohort of the 1970s and of the 1980s respectively. The commercial service is likely to help for only 4 months; about the same duration as for the 1970s cohort (Column 1, Table 3).

Table 3
How Long a Child Spent With Different Care Providers? A Cohort Comparison

(year)	*(Derived from multistate childcare life table)*								
cohort of children	*care status for all mothers(1)*			*for mothers from B1(2)*			*for mothers from B2*		
	f	*w*	*c*	*f*	*w*	*c*	*(3)F*	*w*	*c*
1970s	1.8	3.9	0.3	2.1	3.5	0.5	1.4	4.4	0.2
1980s	2.0	3.8	0.2	2.1	3.7	0.2	2.0	3.9	0.2
1990s	2.6	3.1	0.3	2.7	2.8	0.5	2.4	3.4	0.2

Figures 2a, 2b, and 2c provide the age-and cohort- specific probabilities of being looked after by each "agent." From these we can see the difference in the timing of using different care providers. There is a consensus that across all cohorts, in early childhood, family members were more likely to play a leading role in helping working mothers to balance role-conflicts. The *You er yuan* would become increasingly involved and after the child reached her/his 4th birthday it became the most important extended helping hand to the working mothers from B1 and B2. The commercial services - always in a supportive position for this group of women – tended to decline in importance as a child grows up.

The cohort comparison suggests that, after the reforms, family members have played an increasingly important role in helping the working mothers' childcare affairs. As Figure 2a shows, less than one in two (prob. = 047) 1-year olds born in the 1970s were cared for by grandparents or other female relatives; however, for those who were born in the 1980s, the chance of being cared for by family members increased to more than a third, or 0.77; more than eight in ten (prob. = 0.83) of the 1-year

Figure 2a
Age & Cohort-Specific Probabilities of Children Cared for by Family Members, B1 and B2
Comparing different cohorts
calculation from multi-statechildcare status life table

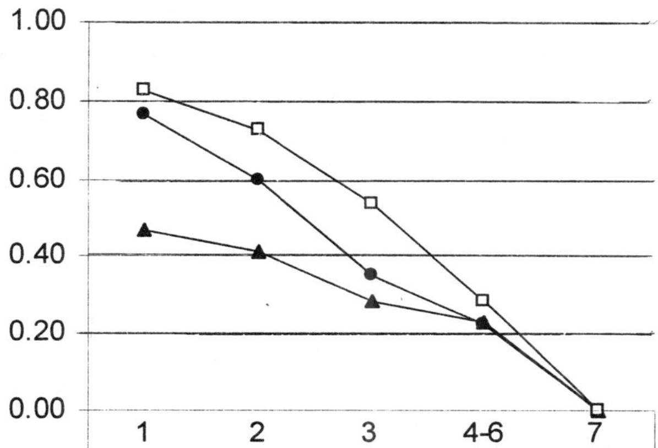

	1	2	3	4-6	7
1970s	0.47	0.41	0.28	0.23	0.00
1980s	0.77	0.60	0.35	0.22	0.00
1990s	0.83	0.73	0.54	0.29	0.00

Figure 2b
Age & Cohort Specific Probabilities of Children Cared for By you ER YUAN, B1 and B2
comparing different cohorts
calculation from multi-statechildcare status life table

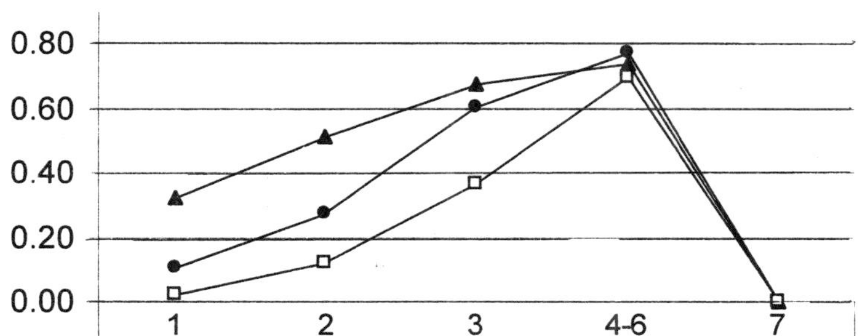

	1	2	3	4-6	7
1970s	0.32	0.51	0.67	0.74	0.00
1980s	0.10	0.28	0.61	0.78	0.00
1990s	0.02	0.12	0.37	0.69	0.00

old born in the 1990s were looked after by family members. In sharp contrast to the increase of family involvement in childcare, as Figure 2b indicates, *You er yuan* has shown a decline in helping working mothers with childcare over the decades, especially for the younger children before the age of 4.

Your er yuan began to play a leading role in childcare after a child reached age 4. We can also see from Figure 2b that about a third (prob. = 0.32) of the 1-year olds born in the 1970s went to the *You er yuan*; the proportion dropped to one in ten for the 1980s' cohort and no mothers of the 1990s' cohort seemed keen to send their one-year olds to the *You er yuan* (prob. = 0.02)! The likelihood that a 2-year old was cared for by *You er yuan* in the 1970s was 0.51. This number declined to 0.28 for the 1980s' cohort and further dropped to 0.12 for the 1990s' cohorts. Similarly, for the 3-year olds, the probability to be cared for by the *You er yuan* declined from 0.67 for the 1970s' cohort to 0.61 for the 1980s' cohort and further to 0.37 for the 1990s' cohort. However, the participation in the *You er yuan* remained at a relatively high level in general. Two thirds to three quarters of the 4-6 year olds were looked after by such welfare provisions.

Commercial services, despite their slow increase, had kept a low profile in the working mothers' childcare arrangements throughout the three decades (Figure 2c). The probability for a

Figure 2c
Age & Cohort-Specific Probabilities of Children Cared for by Commercial Services, B1 and B2
Comparing different cohorts
calculation from multi-statechildcare status life table

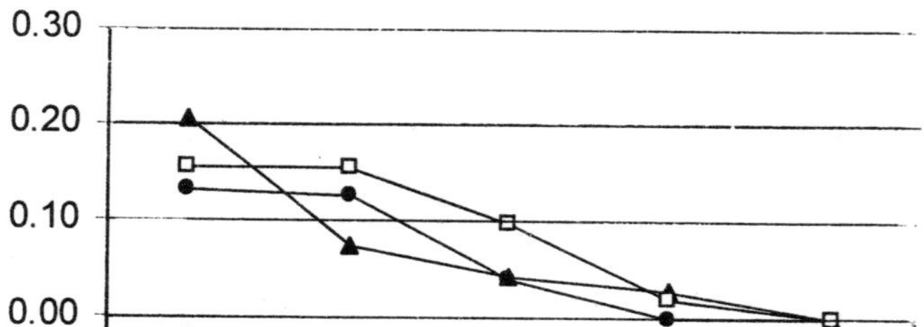

	1	2	3	4-6	7
1970s	0.21	0.07	0.04	0.03	0.00
1980s	0.13	0.13	0.04	0.00	0.00
1990s	0.15	0.15	0.10	0.02	0.00

1-year-old being cared for by commercial services was 0.21 for the 1970s cohort, while the probabilities for the 1980s' cohort and 1990s' cohort were 0.13 and 0.15 respectively. But during age 2 and 3, the 1990s cohort shows a higher probability than the other two cohorts in being cared for by commercial services. We will discuss the use of commercial services by the state female workers below.

Childcare arrangement in the 1990s: comparing the two SOEs. As we mentioned in the previous section, B1 and B2 were one enterprise before they split into two in 1985. After the split, B1, by the time of our survey, had been a profit-making SOE and B2 had been loosing money since the early 1990s. Consequently, B1's employees had been in a better economic situation in terms of wage incomes than their counterparts in B2. In 1997, the average wage in B2 was less than 67 percent of that in B1. In this section we examine if there is any differences in childcare arrangements among the working mothers in the two SOEs given the wage differences. Our calculation on the duration of time spent by a child in different care status (Column 2 and Column 3, Table 3) shows that from age 1-6, a child born to a mother working in B2 would have to stay in the *You er yuan* 7 months longer than a child born to a mother working in B1. And a mother working in B1 is expected to be able to employ commercial services for about 110 days more than a working mother from B2. Figure 3 illustrates age specific probabilities of being cared for by different agents for the children born in the 1990s by the working mothers from B1 and B2. It shows that in the 1990s, working mothers from both B1 and B2 received equivalent help from their family members. But the lower paid women of B2 were more likely to send their children to the *You er yuan* (3-6 percent higher than the mothers from B1) and less likely to pay for the commercial services (on average 5 percent less than the mothers from B1). Such differences could be observed across every age group of children. This indicates that commercial services are more an option for working mothers with better economic conditions, and the welfare facilities are still indispensable for those less successful since the economic reforms.

DISCUSSION

Why has there been a significant rise of family care after the reforms particularly for the under 3-years-olds? Why has the *You er yuan* been the most important "agent" that has provided

Figure 3
Age-Specific Probabilities of Being Cared for By Different Agents, Children of 1990s' Cohort
comparing B1 & B2
calculation from multi-statechildcare status life table

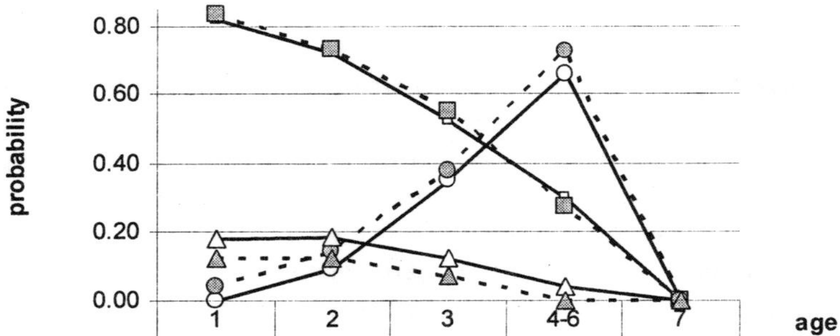

	1	2	3	4-6	7
f, B1	0.82	0.72	0.53	0.30	0.00
f, B2	0.83	0.73	0.55	0.27	0.00
w, B1	0.00	0.09	0.35	0.66	0.00
w, B2	0.04	0.15	0.38	0.73	0.00
c, B1	0.18	0.18	0.12	0.04	0.00
c, B2	0.13	0.13	0.07	0.00	0.00

the longest services especially for the 4-6 years-olds? Why have working mothers in the study used so little commercial services in spite of its rapid growth in the cities after the reforms? In this section we highlight some of the significant factors behind the changes or non-changes of the childcare arrangements by working mothers from B1 and B2. We also draw attention to the new challenges that ordinary working mothers face or will soon face. And finally, in light of the limitations of this study, we point out some directions for further research.

Contextualizing Working Mothers' Childcare Arrangements. (1) *The effect of the "One-child" policy*. The "One-child policy" first introduced in the early 1980s is believed to have had a direct impact to the rise of family care for the children under 3 as well as to the remaining high level of collective care for 4-6 year olds. After 1980 when most of the new born babies were without siblings, parents and grandparents seemed to have determined that they will do every thing in their power to make sure that their "little king" or "little queen" receives the best care possible. The one-to-one based family care is often believed to fit a child's individual needs better than the collective care in a nursery or a kindergarten does. Reflected in this, more than three quarters of the 1-year-olds born in the 1980s were looked after by the grandparents or other female relatives of the family, compared with only fewer than half of the same age group born in the 1970s. The proportion further increased to eight out of ten for the 1990s' cohort (Figure 2a).

Nevertheless, though the family care may be thought to be more advantageous in providing physical care and nurturing, in terms of early education such as language, math, art, music, physical education and general knowledge, the general belief remains that a trained teacher is better than a grandmother. Again in the best interest of the child, as soon as the child reaches the age when the intellectual development is crucial, (s)he is sent to the early learning centers like a kindergarten so that (s)he would not "fall behind the starting line." As shown in our study, from 1970s to 1990s, at least seven out of ten children were educated in the *You er yuan* when they were 4-6 year old (Fig. 2b). Children of wealthier parents are often sent to the expensive, private learning centers with a better educational environment.

(2) *The early retirement practice makes it possible for a family to have a care-giver*. After the economic reform, especially in the 1990s, many work units encouraged employees to take early retirement so as to reduce the over-staffing problem. Many women in their mid-forties or early-fifties left their jobs. Being relatively young and how having enough time, they have been able to look after their grandchildren or the children of their relatives.

(3) *The decline of the state employees' economic status.* From the probabilities of using commercial services (Figure 2c) we find a higher level of usage in the 1970s cohort (prob. = 0.21) than that in the 1980s' cohort (prob. = 0.13) and in the 1990s' cohort (prob. = 0.15). The change in the characteristics of *Bao mu* and the economic statues of state employees before and after the economic reforms may contribute to this. Given that nearly all women at working age were in full-time employment, employing a *Bao mu* to look after the a 1-year-old child was the most common solution before the economic reforms when the mother had to go to work and no relatives were available. On the other hand, before the economic reforms when state workers

were one of the best paid employees, the cost of a *Bao mu* was relatively low to them. On the other hand, as we mentioned before, *Bao mu*'s cost was low. Some of them even did not receive monetary pay at all. After the economic reforms, however, along with the fall of the state worker's economic status and the commercialization of the domestic service, the cost of a *Bao mu* has become less affordable to the state workers.

The challenge: the high dependency on You er yuan versus the decline of the welfare provision. The experience of the women in B1 and B2 shows that the *You er yuan* had been the longest service provider for their children when they were at work. The Multistate Childcare Life Table estimates that, for the 1990s' cohort, *You er yuan* still covered 52 percent of the total care time during the six years of the children's growth from age 1 to 6 (Table 3). It suggests a heavy dependency on the welfare programs by the wage-income based working mothers twenty years after the start of the reforms. However, given the changed the role of SOEs from a government's instrument to an independent economic entity, the shrinkage of the traditional welfare programs seems unavoidable. The increase in the ratio of childcare cost against the average wage in the SOEs, in which female workers account for more than 70 percent of the total staffs, reflects the trend. What happened to the women in B1 and B2 is not an isolate case. The official statistics show that the shrinkage of the old welfare programs is a nation wide phenomenon (*China Statistical Yearbook 2002*). In Beijing itself, the number of work unit based kindergartens dropped from 3056 in 1996 to about 1700 in 2001 (*Beijing Statistical Yearbook 2002*). While the welfare provisions deteriorate, the commercial sector, as we mentioned before, does not yet seem like a realistic option for ordinary working women like those in B1 and B2. The commercial child services only managed to cover about 20 percent of the care of the B1 children and 13 percent of the B2 children in the 1990s' cohort. All this indicates a new challenge that women in China may find it increasingly difficult to remain in employment after becoming mothers due to the lack of affordable childcare services.

Our observation focused on the state female workers and their childcare arrangement through the 1970s to the 1990s. The way in which they arrange their childcare may not be necessarily representative of other female groups. Particularly, as state employees, the income differences between the workers of B1 and B2 do not reflect the growing gap between the rich and poor that has been multiplying since the mid 1990s (Tang 2003). The way in which they arrange their childcare thus cannot represent working mothers nationwide. Further studies on other women's groups, such as women working in the private sector, and self-employed women, etc., are necessary to draw a more complete picture of Chinese working mothers' childcare arrangements.

NOTE

The author thanks The Netherlands Foundation for the Advancement of Tropical Research and Erasmus University of Rotterdam for funding the research. Gratitude also goes to the four anonymous reviewers for their valuable comments on this paper.

REFERENCES

Adams, C.T. , Winston, K.T. (1980), Mothers at Work: Public Policies in the United States, Sweden, and China. London: Longman.

All-China Women's Union & Shaan-xi Women's Union (1991), Xhongguo Funu Tongji Ziliao: 1949-1989 (Statistics on Chinese Women: 1949-1989). Beijing: China Statistical Publishing House.

Andors, P. (1983), The Unfinished Liberation of Chinese Women: 1949-1980. Bloomington, IN: Indiana University Press.

Croll, E. (1983), Chinese Women Since Mao. Zed Books, London.

——. (1994), From Heaven to Earth: Images and Experiences of Development in China. London: Longman.

——. (1995), Changing Identities of Chinese Women: Rhetoric, Experience and Self-perception in Twentieth-century China. Hong Kong: Hong Kong University Press.

Dalsimer, M and Nisonoff, L. (1984). The New Economic Readjustment Policies: Implications for Chinese Urban Working Women. *Review of Radical Political Economics* Vol. 16, 1:17-43.

Eltigani E. (2000), Changes in Family-Building Patterns in Egypt and Morocco: A Comparative Analysis. International Family Planning Perspectives, 73-78.

——. (2001), Childbearing in Five Arab Countries. Studies in Family Planning, 17-24.

Gu, E. (2003), Labor Market Insecurities in China. ILO, Geneva.

ILO (International Labour Organisation) (1995), 1995 Women and the World of Work: the Social Costs of Progress, *http://www.ilo.org/public/english/235press/pktis/women1.html.*

Institute of Population Studies, Chinese Academy of Social Sciences (1994), Women's Status in Contemporary China Result from Sampling Surveys. International Academic Publishers, Beijing. ISBN:7-80003-232-2/C.2.

Jiang, Leiwen (1995), Regional Family Projection in China, *PDOD-Paper*, No. 32. Netherlands Graduate School of Research in Demography, Universiteit van Amsterdam.

Ledent, J. (1980), Multistate (increament-decreament) Life Tables: Movement Versus Transition Perspectives. Environment and Planning, Vol. 12: 533-562.

Mertes K. (2002), 'Little hope' Awaits Women Migrants in China, Northwest Asian Weekly, 3, August 2002.

Onesto, L. (1998), How Collective Childcare Liberated Women in Maoist China. Revolutionary Worker #956, Chicago.

Project of Household Research of Five Cities (1985), Zhongguo chengshi jiating: wu chengshi jiating diaocha baogao ji ziliao huibian (China urban families: research report and data file of household survey in five cities). Jinan: Shandong People's Publishing House.

Robert B. (1994), China Care in China. Children Today, Vol. 23 Issue 2.

Rogers, A. (1973a), The Mathematics of Multiregional Demographic Growth, Environment and Planning, Vol. 5: 3-29.

——. (1973b), The Multi-regional Life Table. *Journal of Mathematical Sociology,* Vol. 3: 127-137.

——. (1975), Introduction to Multiregional Mathematical Demography, Wiley, New York.

Rogers, A. & J. Ledent (1975), Multiregional Population Projection, DP-128, Centre for Mathematical Studies in Economics and Management Science, Northwestern University, Evanston, Illinois.

——. (1976), Increament-Decreament life table: a comment. Demography, Vol. 13: 287-290.

Schoen R. and V. Nelson (1974), Marriage, Divorce and Mortality: A Life Table Analysis, Demography, Vol. 11: 267-290.

Schoen, R. (1975), Constructing Increament-Decreament Life Tables. Demography, Vol. 12: 313-324.

Tan, L. & Li, J (2005), Gender Differences in Informal Employment in China, Women of China English Monthly, June 2005.

Tang, J. (2004), Zhongguo Chenshi pinkun yu fanpinkun baogao (Report on Poverty and Anti-Powerty in Urban China). Beijing Huaxia Publishing House. Translated by M. E. Sharpe. Cited from Chinese Sociology and Anthropology, Vol. 36 nos. 2-3.

Won, J. (2004), Withering Away of the Iron Rice Bowl? The Reemployment Project of Post-Socialist China. Studies in Comparative International Development, Vol.39, No. 2: 71-93.

World Bank (2005), World Development Indicators, http:// www.worldbank.org/data/wdi2005/ wditext / Cover.htm

Xie, H. (1990), The Changing Role and Status of Women in China, *http: / / www.1990institute.org / publications / pubs / ISUPAP8.html*

Xu, A. (2005), The Relationship between Female's Participation in Housework and Satisfaction to Wedlock, Women of China (English Monthly), June 2005.

Xu, Y. (2000), Forecasting Labor Supply in Urban China: Integrating Demographic Dynamics and Socioeconomic Transition, *Interim Report IR-00-011*, International Institute for Applied Systems Analysis, Laxenburg, Austria.

Zeng Y. (1991a), Family Dynamics in China: A Life-Table Analysis. Madison, WI: University of Wisconsin Press.

——. (1991b), A Comparative Study on Changes in Family in Chinese Countryside and Cities. In Fertility in China. Proceedings of the International Seminar on China's in-Depth Fertility Survey, Beijing, February 13-17, 1990. Published by the International Statistical Institute, Voorburg, The Netherlands.

——. (1993), *Renkou fenxi fangfa yu yingyong* (Methodology and application of demographic analysis). Beijing: Peking University Press.

——. (1995), *Bashi Niandai de Lihun Shuiping Jiqi Biandong Qushi* (The Level and Trend of Divorce in China in the 1980s), in Zeng y. *et al. edt.* Zhongguo Bashi Niandai Lihun yanjiu (A Study on Divorce in the 1980s in China). Beijing: Peking University Press.

Zha, R.Ch. (1991), Some Analysis of the Age at First Marriage and Fertility Level of Women of Five Provinces and One Municipality, in Fertility in China. Proceedings of the International Seminar on China's in-Depth Fertility Survey, Beijing, February 13-17, 1990. Published by the International Statistical Institute, Voorburg, The Netherlands.

ATTITUDES TOWARDS THE ELDERLY IN CHINA

Xiaolin Xie and Yan Xia

5

INTRODUCTION AND LITERATURE REVIEW

Traditional Chinese culture emphasizes the importance and value of older people. These attitudes are fostered by the Confucian philosophy that undergirds much of Chinese culture and by China's traditional multi-generational family structure. However, since the late 1970's, China has undergone rapid social changes. Generally, modernization and urbanization are believed to promote value systems that either equalize age groups or result in lower status for older people (Cowgill, 1975). In addition, rapid economic development, greater access and job mobility for young adults, and easing of severe housing constraints have resulted in the decrease of three- generation households. Therefore, it will be of interest to examine attitudes toward older people between young adults and baby boomers against the cultural and social backdrops.

Changes in Household Structures

The long enduring Chinese cultural ethic that pays homage to respecting seniors and age hierarchy comes through in adages such as "the elder is a treasure in the family." The elderly, therefore, are theoretically accorded the highest position in the family hierarchy, respected, and honored by the young (Uba, 1994). The notion of filial piety is also manifested in support for older people via the formation of three-generation households. In comparative terms, Chinese families have had (and continue to have) a fairly high rate of three-generation households. For example, studies show that 40-50 percent of urban Chinese families lived in three-generation households in the mid-1980s (Hu and Ye, 1991; Unger, 1993), compared to the U.S. figure of approximately 18 percent (Crimmins and Ingegneri, 1990).

Some researchers have attributed the high occurrence of three-generation households to the government's lack of support and interest in expanding the urban housing market between the 1950s and early 1980s (Chen, 1996; Unger, 1993). According to this interpretation, the shortage of housing forced many adult children to live with their parents. Other researchers have argued that three-generation households associated with these developments mainly served the needs of adult children (Aquilino, 1990; Davis-Friedmann, 1991). Similarly, Knodel et. al., (1992) have pointed out that three-generation households in Thailand were largely child-centered. Accordingly, some older people stated their preferences in living arrangement. Treas and Wang (1993) found that 79 percent of men and 65 percent of women aged 60 and older in the metropolitan of Shanghai favored a separate residence. Though in separate residence, they also preferred living in the vicinity of at least one of their adult children. Some researchers coined the term "networked family" to describe the intergenerational linkages to provide support when needed (Pan and Ruan, 1995; Xu, 1995). Chen and Silverstein's (2000) study also revealed that the number of children and the gender of children were not significantly related to elder support, rather, having at least one proximate child increased the likelihood of receiving support.

Though three-generation households may be one traditional arrangement that manifests deference, respect and support to the elderly, Zhan (2004a) found that living arrangement impacted contemporary Chinese young adult's attitudes toward filial responsibility in a negative manner. Young adults from three-generation households reported to be less committed to their sense of obligation to elder care. Take together, Chinese families have long been described as a corporate kin group that cared for the welfare of all family members and were bound by common goals and interests (Tu, Freedman, and Wolf, 1993). However, as a result of the broadening of housing construction, the traditional Chinese family living arrangement – the three-generation household - may no longer be the norm. Older people in China today are more likely to maintain separate living household from their adult children than in the past (Chen and Silverstein, 2000).

Gender

Yang (1996) notes that in the traditional Chinese family, support for the elderly was not uniform; rather, it varied by gender. Sons were usually expected to support their parents financially. Gui (1988) in his study found that in rural China, sons provided the most in medical care, spouses second, and daughters the third. Likewise, in other parts of China, of those legally responsible for the elder, 30 percent were oldest sons, 10 percent were oldest daughters, and 31 percent other children (Chinese Population Information and Research Center, 1990). Zhan and Montgomery (2003) investigated the changing dynamics of caregiving in urban China against the backdrops of economic reforms and cultural emphasis of *xiao* (filial piety). Their study showed "a decline in the patrilocal tradition of caregiving." Taking care of the elderly was shifting from being the sons' to daughters' responsibility. However, the authors were concerned that these female caregivers, with fewer children, more financially dependent, and more likely to live longer, may face challenges in future elder care themselves.

Studies on this topic in other cultures also pointed toward a female caregiving pattern. Neal and Ingersoll (1997) in the US found daughters devoted more time and were more likely to be primary caregivers. When comparing support for parents with dementia in Korea and the U.S. Lee and Sung (1997) found that daughters-in-law were the main caregivers in Korea whereas in the U.S., they were major caregivers. The former group reported a higher score on filial obligation and the latter group reported a more affectionate relationship with their parents.

The notion of having daughters as the caregivers is undergoing changes in China. China was reported to have one of the highest female employment rates. With the one child per family policy, parents in urban China were willing to invest in their only child's education, be it a boy or girl. For example, Tsui and Rich (2002) revealed no significant differences in parental expectations and investment, and math performance for boys and girls from only-child families. The greater education opportunity granted to women today and the potential for economic mobility would likely continue to change the traditional Chinese housing arrangements and especially contribute to more women living separately from their parents'.

Attitudes Toward The Elderly

Though Asian cultures are portrayed in the west as showing favorable attitudes toward older people (Tobin, 1987), attitudes toward the elderly may be changing as a result of social and economic changes. Zhan (2004a) reported that children from one-child families were less committed to elder care when career considerations impinged on them than those from multiple children families. Specifically, the former were less willing to co-reside with their parents than the latter. Of interest, investment in the education of an only child may not be positively related to future elder care (Zhan, 2004b). The increasing economic well-being of urban families, which has, among other things, allowed parents to invest in their child, has been an impetus for young adults to move out of their home communities.

Given these trends in China and elsewhere in Asia, there is concern about the decline of family support for the elderly and the need to reiterate the importance of filial piety and broadening public services. In Korea, filial piety included cohesive family relationships, family obligation, interdependence between members, and pooling of resources for the family's well-being (Sung, 2000). Sung (2004) found that in Korea, youth practiced elder respect by living together with elders, following their advice on marriage, accepting their values and lifestyles, and consulting them over personal and family issues. Despite the rapid social and economic development in China, there is very little research that has focused on people's attitudes toward the elderly. A review of research done in the west provided some updated information. In the U.S., research on attitudes toward the elderly (age 60 and older), have yielded inconsistent results. Among them, many unveil stereotypically negative attitudes (Hummert, 1990; Kite, et al, 1991); some revealed neutral attitudes (Bell and Stanfield, 1973) and a few found positive attitudes (Kite and Johnson, 1988).

Palmore (1982) suggested that negative stereotypes of older people were prevalent in American society. However, more recent studies found that negative attitudes towards older people were not as common as previously indicated (Slotterback and Saarnio, 1996). This may be due to a couple reasons. First, the growth in the population of older people in the U.S. increased their visibility and the contact between younger and older generation. Second, the media, a major force in socializing young people, appeared to project a different picture of older people than it did in previous decades. Bell (1992) documented that older people were being portrayed in a more positive manner on television than they had been in the past. Furthermore, these attitudes appeared to vary with age and the sex of the respondents. Older adults seemed to have more favorable attitudes toward their own peer than younger adults did (Baily, 1991). However, even in older adult cohorts, Seccombe and Ishii-Kuntz (1991) revealed that the youngest cohort (55-64) had the more pessimistic view of growing older than the oldest cohort (age 85+).

In a study of college students' attitudes toward the older men and women found that college age respondents, particularly males, were stereotypically gender-specific (Hawkins, 1996). College aged males perceived elderly males to be untidy, sad, and dependent. Although they had a more positive attitude toward elderly men than they did toward elderly women whom they saw as unproductive and dependent, they saw older women as nurturing and older men as more intellectually competent and autonomous (Canetto et. al., 1995).

Studies on contact with older people influences people's attitudes reached conflicting results. Hawkins (1996) found that students who had prior experience with older people were significantly more likely to have positive attitudes toward older adults than those who did not have any contact. However, Chang, Chang and Shen's (1985) study revealed no significant difference in attitudes toward older people between American Chinese who maintained close contact with their grandparents and those with no contact. They concluded that it was not contact with older people per se, but rather, it was the quality of the contact that mattered. Zhan (2004b) found that among young adults from one-child family, close contacts with grandparents were negatively associated with their willingness for parent care in the future. In sum, attitudes toward older people in China are under-researched. With the decreasing size of families, and increasing number of people reaching retirement age, it will be of interest to investigate younger adults' attitudes toward the elderly.

METHOD

In studying attitudes toward the elderly in China, we specifically focus on the perspectives of college students and baby boomers toward older people. We also investigated if household structures (nuclear families vs. three-generation households), and gender, would influence one's attitudes toward the elderly. Kogan's Attitude towards Older People (Kogan, 1961) was used for this study.

Participants

Three hundred and five students from two different universities and 85 baby boomers from two state-run companies in Southern China participated in this study. Each university had an enrollment of about 10,000 students. The two companies had about 1000 employees at the time the survey was conducted. Both groups were informed of the purpose of the study. The college students completed the survey in the classroom setting. The baby boomers filled out the survey in their homes or offices, (some were allowed to bring the survey home and brought it back the next day if they did not have time to fill it out at work). Both sets of data were collected in the summer of 2000 using a convenient sampling method in Guangzhou, a metropolitan city in southern China with a population of 7 millions. Our student sample consisted of 71 (23 percent) males and 230 (75 percent) females. One hundred and forty-five (48 percent) were from a three-generation family, and 153 (50 percent) were from a nuclear family. Three-generation household was defined as having three generations living in the family in the past year for the baby boomers, and for the college students, it referred to the family they were living with before they left for college. The students' ages ranged from 18 to 24, and none of them were married when the study was conducted.

In the baby boomer sample, 40 (47 percent) were males, and 44 (52 percent) were females. Seventeen (20 percent) were from three-generational households, 61 (72 percent) were from nuclear families, and the rest (8 percent) were missing data.

Instrument

The Kogan 'Attitudes Toward Old People' Survey was used for this study. Although this survey was first used in the 1960s, it was chosen for this study because of its content validity. There were 34 items in this survey, with half of the 34 items phrased positively, while the other half negatively. This split-half survey has reported reliability coefficients ranging from .66 to .85

(Kogan, 1961). For this study, the reliability coefficient for all 34 items was .75, indicating a moderate level of internal consistency. Participants are asked to rate the items in a six point Likert scale ranging from "strongly disagree (1)," "disagree (2)," "somewhat disagree (3)," "somewhat agree (4)," "agree (5)," and "strongly agree (6)."

One key issue in cross-cultural study is measurement equivalency (Buchko, 1994). In order to avoid or reduce nonequivalent measurements in the English and Chinese versions, the back translation technique was used after the scales were translated into Chinese. The first author, a native speaker of Chinese, translated the instruments into Chinese. The English version of these instruments was then translated back into Chinese by two researchers whose first language is Chinese and second language is English. The researchers compared the translations, checked for discrepancies, and made changes wherever appropriate.

Data Analysis

A new dependent variable was created by averaging the scores for all 34 items, with the 17 negatively phrased items reversely coded. Therefore, the higher the mean, the more favorable the attitude toward older people it denoted. Cohort groups and household structures were both dummy-coded (baby boomer as 1 and college student as 0; nuclear family household as 1 and three-generation household as 0). An Analysis of Covariance (ANCOVA) was conducted using General Linear Regression on SPSS to detect any effects of cohort groups, gender, and household structure, and interaction between cohorts (college students vs. baby boomers) and household structure (nuclear family household vs. three-generation household) when gender was controlled. Two stepwise hierarchical regression analyses were executed to determine the relative strength of the predictors (gender, household structure, and cohort) of the attitude score. One was performed with a specific order and the other one without.

RESULTS

Due to the different sample sizes for college students and for baby boomers, Levene's test of equality of error variances was performed. None was significant ($F=.465$, $p=.71$); indicating the homogeneity assumption was not violated, and the results of the following tests were reliable.

Analysis of Covariance (ANCOVA)

Analysis of Covariance (ANCOVA) was performed with cohort and household structure as independent variable and gender as covariate. No significant effect was detected for interaction between cohort groups and household structure, and further confirmed that homogeneity across the comparison groups was not violated. Cohort group was highly significant while household structure was not significant (p = .06) when gender was controlled. Gender was observed significant (See Tables 1 and 2).

Table 1
Summary for Analysis of Covariance

Source	*df*	*F*
Gender (covariate)	1	3.86*
Household structure (H)	1	3.44
Cohorts (C)	1	10.90***
H x C	1	.002
Error	370	(.159)

Table 2
Estimated Cell Means for ANCOVA

Source			*Cohorts* *Student*	*Boomer*
			3.84 (.03)	4.03 (.05)
Household	Extended	3.99 (.05)	3.87 (.03)	4.07 (.09)
Structure	Nuclear	3.88 (.03)	3.76 (.03)	3.96 (.05)
Gender	Female	3.91 (.04)	3.90 (.05)	4.02 (.08)
	Male	3.96 (.05)	3.79 (.03)	4.03 (.07)

Note: Standard Error in the parenthesis.

Stepwise Hierarchical Regress Analyses

Two stepwise hierarchical regression analyses were conducted: (1) to determine if cohort was still a significant predictor with gender and household structure being controlled, and gender, household structure, and cohort were entered in order in the stepwise regression; and (2) to determine the relative importance of the predictors (i.e. gender, household structure, and cohort) of the attitude score. (See Table 3). Results showed that cohort group had an effect independent of gender and household structure and had the strongest influence on attitudes toward older people.

Table 3
Stepwise Hierarchical Regression Analysis for Variables Predicting Attitudes toward Older People

Variables	*Parameter Estimates*				
	B	*SB*	*β*	R^2	*“R^2 (p)*
Without Specified Order					
Step 1					
Cohort	.192	.051	.091***		
				.036	.036 (p<.001)
Step 2					
Cohort	.218	.052	.217***		
Structure	-.097	.043	-.118*		
				.05	.014 (p=.023)
Step 3					
Cohort	.20	.053	.199***		
Structure	-.112	.043	-.136**		
Gender	-.093	.047	-.103*		
				.06	.01 (p=.05)
With Specified Order					
Step 1					
Gender	-.105	.047	-.116*		
				.013	.013(p=.025)
Step 2					
Gender	-.071	.047	-.079		
Structure	.175	.052	.174*		
				.042	.029(p=.001)
Step 3					
Gender	-.093	.047	-.103*		
Structure	.200	.053	.199***		
Cohort	-.112	.043	-.136**		
				.059	.017(p=.010)

Note: *p < / =.05; ** p </= .01; *** p </= .001.

DISCUSSION

Analysis of Covariance (ANCOVA) revealed that cohort (baby boomers vs. college students) was significant in predicting attitudes toward the elderly in our sample with baby boomers (M=4.03) reporting more positive attitudes than students (M=3.84). This finding is consistent with Bailey's (1991) study in the U.S. that older adults seemed to have more favorite attitudes toward their peer group than younger adults.

Interestingly, ANCOVA and stepwise regression when gender was controlled produced mixed results regarding household structure. Household structure (three-generation households vs. nuclear family households) was found to be non-significant by ANCOVA and by stepwise regression when gender was controlled, whereas it was a significant factor in stepwise regression when gender was not controlled. It may be that gender and household structure were confounded in this sample, as the majority of the three-generation households were from the student sample. In the baby boomer sample, only 17 (20 percent) were from three-generation households, whereas in the student sample, 145 (48 percent) were from three-generation households. In addition, a majority of the college students were female (75 percent).

Furthermore, the non-significance with gender being controlled may be attributed to the differences between the two groups in the regions the participants came from. The baby boomer's data set was collected in Guangzhou where the housing market has been expanding significantly in the past two decades, thus, allowing many adults to purchase their own housing units, and decreasing the number of multigenerational households. The student participants, though studying in Guangzhou, did not come from the same city; rather, they were from various parts of the country where housing markets do vary. Consistent with Zhan's (2004b) study, students living with their grandparents may witness how their parents took care of their grandparents and were more realistic of what caregiving entailed. They may also resent the loss of space and privacy due to more people living in the same house. Hence, in this study, living in a three-generation household did not significantly increase their positive attitude score toward the elderly.

Gender was found to be significant with male participants (M=3.96) reporting more positive attitudes toward older people than their female counterparts (M=3.91). As aforementioned, it is highly plausible that with females generally socialized to be the care givers, and more involved in the daily care of elderly family members, they are therefore more aware of the caregiving hardships. Their perceptions of what caregiving demands may well dampen their positive attitudes toward older people.

There was no significant interaction between cohort and household structure indicating neither one was dependent on the other. To determine the relative strength of each of the predictors (gender, cohort, and household structure), two stepwise hierarchical regression analyses were performed. The first regression analysis was conducted with a specific order – gender, cohort, and household structure, while the second analysis was done without any specific order. The cohort variable was found to be the strongest predictor independent of gender and household structure.

When each of the 34 items was examined individually, some interesting differences between the two cohorts were revealed. On the one hand, college students agreed more to the following statements: "Most old people get set in their ways and are unable to change," "One of the most interesting and entertaining qualities of most old people is their accounts of their past experiences," "Most old people spend too much time prying into affairs of others and giving unsought advice," "Most old people are constantly complaining about the behavior of the younger generation," and "Old people have too much power in business and politics." This last statement may reflect the specific feature of gerontocracy in China. However, this topic is beyond of the scope of this paper.

On the other hand, baby boomers agreed more to the following statements "Most old people are cheerful, agreeable, and good humored," "One seldom hears old people complaining about the behavior of the younger generation," "Most old people are really no different from anybody else: they are as easy to understand as younger people," "People grow wiser with the coming of old age," and "Most old people would prefer to continue working just as long as they possibly can rather be dependent on anybody else." The last statement may reflect baby boomers' desire to continue working past the mandatory retirement age, which was set at 60 for males, and 55 for females in many state-run enterprises. At the same time, it also reflected baby boomers' concern about retirement security. The baby boomer data set was collected from state-owned enterprises at the time when this system was gradually being dismantled because of limited resources the state had. As a result, many baby boomers would face loss of support in medical care and housing subsidies, and possible loss of pension. Therefore, it is no surprise that more baby boomers than college students concurred with that statement.

CONCLUSION

Confucianism is undoubtedly deeply rooted in Chinese culture, and among other things, it underscores family relations and family hierarchy. One tenet in Confucianism, filial piety has been manifested in the traditional living arrangements (e.g., three-generation households), where support across generations is accessible. However, with the expansion of economic opportunities, a growing housing market in urban China, and with greater job mobility for young adults, three-generation households are on the decline. In this study, only 20 percent of baby boomers residing in Guangzhou were in the traditional three-generation households. They also reported more positive attitudes toward the elderly than college students. Further, male participants reported more positive attitudes than their female counterparts.

In light of the one child per family policy, and the high employment rate for females in China, the family may not be the panacea for elder care in the future. This is especially true today when many parents in urban China seemingly invest in their only child's education, and accordingly, provide their only child an opportunity to pursue opportunities in other parts of country, or abroad. Hence, elder care is no longer an isolated family issue. Clearly, these developments raise some critical housing and elderly care policy concerns. In particular, there is compelling reason for policy makers to consider and incorporate state-funded programs for the elderly as into the current model of family care. Efforts to establish a universal social security and health care system, and to develop various social programs for older people may need to be accelerated.

NOTES

The small sample size for this study, especially, for the baby boomer group, and the non-random sampling method obviously limits the generalizability of this study to its larger population. Future studies should involve larger samples from different locations.

REFERENCES

Aquilino, W. (1990), The Likelihood of Parent-Child Coresidence Effects of Family Structure and Parental Characteristics. *Journal of Marriage and the Family,* 52: 405-19.

Baily, W. T. (1991), Knowledge, Attitude and Psychosocial Development of Young and Old Adults. Educational Gerontology, 17: 269-274.

Bell, B. D., and Stanfield, G. G. (1973), Chronological Age in Relation to Attitudinal Judgments: An Experimental Analysis. *Journal of Gerontology,* 28: 491-496.

Bell, J. (1992). In Search of a Discourse on Aging: The Elderly on Television. Gerontologist, 32: 305-311.

Buchko, A. A. (1994), Conceptualization and measurement of environmental uncertainty: An assessment of the miles and snow perceived environment uncertainty scale. *Academy of Management Journal,* 37: 410-425.

Canetto, S.S., Kaminiski, P. L., and Felicio, D. M. (1995), Typical and optimal aging in women and men: Is there a double standard? *International Journal of Aging and Human Development,* 40: 187-207.

Chang, B.L., Chang, A.F., and Shen, Y. (Spring, 1985). Attitudes toward aging in the United States and Taiwan. *Journal of Comparative Family Studies,* 15 (1): 109-130.

Chen, J. (1996). Old Age Support and Intergenerational Relation in Urban China: Maintenance of Obligations between Older Parents and Children. Ph.D. Dissertation, Department of Sociology, University of Michigan, Ann Arbor, MI.

Chen, X., and Silverstein, M. (2000), Intergenerational Social Support and the Psychological Well-Being of Older Parents in China. Research on Aging, 22 (1): 43065.

Chinese Population Information and Research Center (1990). Beijing: Beijing Institute of Economics Press.

Cowgill, D. O. (1975), Aging and Modernization: a Revision of the Theory. In J. Gubrium (Ed.), Late life: Communities and Environmental Policy. Springfield, IL.: Charles Thomas.

Crimmins, E., and Ingegneri, D. (1990), Interaction and Living Arrangement of Older Parents and their Children. Research on Aging, 12: 3-35.

David-Friedmann, D. (1991), Long lives: Chinese Elderly and the Communist Revolution. Cambridge: Harvard University Press.

Gui, S. X. (1988), A Report from Mainland China: Status and Needs of Rural Elderly in the Suburbs of Shanghai. *Journal of Cross-Cultural Gerontology,* 3: 149-167.

Hawkins, M.J. (1996), College Students' Attitudes Towards Elderly Persons. Educational Gerontology, 22: 271-279.

Hu, R., and Ye, N. (1991), The Nine-City Survey on Aging in 1988. Tianjin: Tianjin Educational Press.

Hummert, M.L. (1990), Multiple stereotypes of elderly and young adults: A comparison of structure and evaluation. Psychological and Aging, 5: 182-193.

Kite, M.E., Deaux, K., and Miele, M. (1991), Stereotypes of Young and Old: Does Age Outweigh gender? Psychological and Aging, 6: 19-27.

Kite, M.E., and Johnson, B. T. (1988), Attitudes Toward Older and Younger Adults: A Meta-Analysis. Psychological and Aging, 3: 233-244.

Knodel, J., Chayovan, N., and Siriboon S. (1992). The Impact of Fertility Decline on Familial Support for the Elderly: An Illustration from Thailand. Population and Development Review, 18: 79-103.

Kogan, N. (1961), Attitudes Toward Old People: The Development of a Scale and an Examination of Correlates. *Journal of Abnormal and Social Psychology,* 62 (1): 44-54.

Lee, Y.R., and Sung, K. T. (1997), Cultural Differences in Caregiving Motivations for Demented Parents: Korean Caregivers versus American Caregivers. *International Journal of Aging and Human Development,* 44: 115-127.

Neal, M., and Ingersoll, B. (1997), Gender and Relationship Differences in Caregiving Patterns and Consequences among Employed Caregivers. Gerontologist, 37 (6): 804-816.

Palmore, E. B. (1982), Attitudes Toward the Aged: What we Know and Need to know. Research on Aging, 4: 333-348.

Pan, Y.K., and Ruan, D. Q. (1995), Chinese Urban Family Networks. *Zhejiang Academic Journal,* 3: 66-71.

Seccombe, K., and Ishii-Kuntz, M. (1991), Perceptions of Problems Associated with aging: Comparisons among Four Older Age Cohorts. The Gerontologist, 4: 527-533.

Sloterback, C. S., and Saarnio, D.A. (1996), Attitudes Toward Older Adults Reported by Young Adults: Variation Based on Attitudinal Task and Attribute Categories. Psychology and Aging, 11 (4): 563-571.

Sung, K.T. (2004), Elder Respect Among Young Adults: A Cross-Cultural Study of Americans and Koreans. *Journal of Aging Studies,* 18: 215-230.

Sung, K.T. (2000), An Asian Perspective on Aging East and West: Filial Piety and Changing Families. In Bengtson, V.L., Kim, K., Myers, G.C., and Eun, K.S. (Eds.), Aging in East and West: Family, States, and Elderly. Springer Publishing Company.

Tobin, J.J. (1987), The American Idealization of Old Age in Japan. The Gerontologist, 27: 53-58.

Treas, J., and Wang, W. (1993), Of deeds and contracts: Filial Piety Perceived in Contemporary Shanghai. In V. Bengston and Achenbaum, A. (Eds.), The changing contract across generations. Aldine de Gruyter.

Tsui, M., and Rich, L. (2002), The Only Child and Educational Opportunity for Girls in Urban China. Gender and Society, 16 (1): 74-92.

Tu, E.J., Freeman, V.A., and Wolf, D.A. (1993), Kinship and Family Support in Taiwan, Research on Aging, 15: 465-86.

Uba, L. (1994), Asian Americans: Personality Patterns, Identity, and Mental Health. New York: Guilford Press.

Unger, J. (1993), Urban Families in the Eighties. In Davis, D., and Hareel, S. (eds.) Chinese Families in the Post-Mao era. Berkeley: University of California Press.

Yang, H. (1996), The Distributive Norm of Monetary Support to Older Parents: A look at a Township. China. *Journal of Marriage and the Family,* 58 (2): 404-416.

Xu, A. J. (1995), The Situation and Changes of Urban Family and Social Networks. Shanghai *Academy of Social Sciences Academic Journal,* 2: 77-85.

Zhan, H. J. (2004a), Socialization or Social Structure: Investigating Predictors of Attitudes toward Filial Responsibility Among Chinese Urban Youth From One and Multiple-Child Families. The International Journal of Aging and Human Development, 59 (2): 105-124.

Zhan, H. J. (2004b), Willingness and Expectations: Intergenerational Differences in Attitudes Toward Filial Responsibility. China. *Journal of Marriage and Family Review,* 36 (1/2): 175-200.

Zhan, H. J., and Montgomery, R. J. V. (2003). Gender and Elder Care in China: The Influence of Filial Piety and Structural Constraints. Gender and Society, 17 (2): 209-220.

THE EMERGENCE OF THE NUCLEAR FAMILY IN MEXICO

6

Rosario Esteinou

INTRODUCTION

The nuclear family in Mexico currently constitutes the main form of familial organization. The recent censuses of 1990 and 2000 registered that 73.9 per cent and 66.9 per cent respectively of all homes are nuclear (INEGI, 2003). In spite of this majority presence, we still know little about its characteristics and its historical development. Historians have indicated that the nuclear family has already been existent since the colonial period (16th to 19th centuries), but there has been no identification of its similarities or differences with the contemporary nuclear family or with the Western nuclear family described in classical sociology, for instance by Parsons (1955). The aim of the present article is to analyze the emergence of the nuclear family in Mexico and to point to its particularities and differences in comparison with the Western nuclear family. This exploration departs from three analytic dimensions: family structure, family relationships, and kinship relationships. I propose the thesis that, contrary to what has been asserted by some historians, the nuclear family from a socio-cultural viewpoint did not emerge during the colonial period.

THE FAMILY: THREE ANALYTIC DIMENSIONS

Marzio Barbagli (1987) has pointed to three dimensions according to which the concept 'family' has been conceptualized or the reality of family life has been understood in the international literature: family structure, family relationships, and kinship relationships. The first comprises the group of persons that live under the same roof, the breadth and composition of this aggregate of cohabitants, and the rules according to which it is formed, transformed and divided. The second includes affective and authority relations within this group of cohabitants, the modes through which these interact and treat each other, and the emotions and feelings that prove one to the other. The third refers to the relations existing between distinct groups of cohabitants who have kinship ties, the frequency with which they see each other, help each other, and work out and follow joint strategies to increase or at least conserve their economic resources, their power, and their prestige.

The precision of these three dimensions has been the result of various debates at the international level around the definition of the concept of family and the historical forms it has assumed. As part of these debates, the relationship to be established between these three dimensions has been discussed, as until the 1960s and the 1970s most family sociology assumed one particular form of this relationship. The basic formulation prevalent at the time can be summarized as follows: In the transition from a simple society to another, complex one, and from traditional historical social formations to modern and therefore contemporary ones, the family changed from extended to nuclear. Within this transformation, the family changed as much in its structure as in its relationships and its functions. From the point of view of functions, departing from a polyfunctional structure (unit of production and consumption, bearer of the cultural mechanisms for the transmission of norms and values, for the social integration of its members, for the primary and secondary socialization of new generations, for the control over property, and for the satisfaction of the necessities of the cohabiting subjects), the family lost capacities in many of its functions, which thus were assumed by other, external agencies (school, factory, the market in a general sense, the church, etc.), and it came to be characterized by an eminently expressive function (stabilization of the adult personality & primary socialization of the children). The increase in the division of labor, with the related process of functional specialization of the subsystems that constituted the social system, and the Industrialization made up the main factors of influence regarding the transformation of the family. The thesis of the existence of a process of progressive simplification of the family structures originated from the work of Durkheim (1975) and found conceptual continuity with the work of Parsons (1955).

However, the postulate of the emergence of the nuclear family did not concern only the emergence of one particular type of structure. Another element implied in this evolutionist conceptualization is that the nuclear structure requires a particular ordering and content of the intra-familial relationships. This means that according to the degree to which the family acquires this structure, certain family relationships are configured within it, and they come to be dissociated from kinship relationships. It is evident that this model supposed that the three highlighted dimensions very clearly corresponded to each other. This meant – as Barbagli (1987) has pointed out– that it was enough to study one of them to acquire data on the other dimensions as well.

This model came to be questioned by different disciplines. Within anthropology, the critique by Lévi-Strauss (1995), for instance, hit the evolutionist model hard. Within sociology, the studies of König (1970), Sennett (1984), and McLaughlin (1971), as well as the debate between Litwak (1960a; 1960b) and Parsons (1980) made evident the limitations of the Parsonian conceptual framework. They showed, among other points, the importance of social class and of kinship ties for the survival of the nuclear family in urban contexts.

The studies realized within historical demography proved quite rich and fruitful in their questioning of this evolutionist model of the history of family forms. The most important contribution came from Laslett (1972), who showed that the nuclear family, from the point of view of its structure, had preceded industrialization by centuries. Another interesting contribution originated from another branch of historiography. Authors such as Ariés (1987), Shorter (1975), and Stone (1983) explored extensively the symbolic and cultural meaning which founding a family possesses for men and women in the transition from medieval to modern, contemporary society. Their studies focus especially on the dimension of internal family relationships. For these authors, it is possible to recognize- beyond and in spite of the structural characteristics of the family in various European contexts-an element of socio-cultural fracture between the end of the 16th century and the beginning of the 17th. It had a profound impact on family relationships, modifying affective and authority relationships between the sexes and the generations; they slowly acquired a more sentimental character in terms of 'privacy'. Consequently, the emergence of internal family relationships of the nuclear type should be assumed to have a place in the pre-industrial period.

According to Stone (1983), the following changes took place in family relationships during the transition from the traditional extended family to the modern nuclear one: First, the liberation from the control exercised by the community and kin; second, the passage from a system of marriages agreed by the parents and based on social and economic interests to a system of spousal choice based on physical attraction and love; third, a change in the relationship between the spouses from coldness and distance to affective warmth, intimacy and erotic passion; fourth, the transition of the relation between parents and children from indifference to parental care and concern; and fifth, the increasingly egalitarian connotations of the relations between sexes and generations as well as the increasing autonomy of individual family members.

Given this questioning of the outlined model of the history of family forms, we can conclude the following: First, industrialization, instead of creating the nuclear family, contributed to its diffusion among social classes and strata showing distinct modes of organization up to the point of transforming it into the dominant family form of modern society. Second, the discussed three dimensions do not maintain a univocal relationship among each other, so that it becomes important to analyze the content of each of them and to define the relationships existing between them on this base. A nuclear structure may contain diverse forms of family relationships, and an extended family might be rooted in emotion-based individualism, in the mentality of the market, or in romantic love. Last, it is furthermore necessary to take into account the relations with and the role played by kinship relationships. Keeping in mind these three dimensions as well as the relations to be established between them in each case, I will now try to reconstruct the process of the emergence of the nuclear family in Mexico.

THE EMERGENCE OF THE NUCLEAR FAMILY IN MEXICO

In the area of historiography in Mexico, the study of the family is fairly recent and has assumed a rather subordinate position in the analysis of other problem areas, as Gonzalbo (1998) has indicated. Furthermore, the exploration of its historical development has not been very receptive to the parameters orienting debates at the international level. This has entailed that the thesis of the nuclearization of the family has been appropriated in a partial and superficial form. In part, this is due to the novelty of this field of study in Mexico, the scarcity and thematic dispersion of the studies that have been conducted, and the difficulty of locating sources on relevant issues. To these problems, one should add the difficulty of incorporating a conceptual framework guiding the organization of information and providing interpretive parameters. Effectively, many previous studies have focused on description and lack and an interpretive frame.

The current state of research in Mexico therefore does not allow us to elaborate a history of the development of the family as it has been done in other Western countries. Nevertheless, the existing studies allow us to reconstruct some of its most important features. This reconstruction to be presented here is grounded in the above mentioned three analytic dimensions and in the theses and debates brought forward in the international literature.

During the prehispanic period, i.e., prior to the Conquest by the Spanish in the 16th century, and the first decades of the colony, considerable proportions of the indigenous families showed an extended structure, the size of their homes was considerable (Carrasco, 1993; 1982), and kinship relationships had a very important presence and weight (López Austin, 1982). The configuration of this type of family structure corresponded to certain rules of family formation, according to which new marriages or unions maintained their residence in the parents' home-generally patrilocally–and after a few years established themselves independently after acquiring the recognition of the community and access to a plot of land of their own (Gonzalbo, 1998). However, this independence was relative in so far as the ties with the family of origin, i.e., the kinship relationships, were strong. This showed itself in different ways. When they set up their own home, they did so around the same court (*patio*), plot, or at least close to the parents' home. They maintained work-related connections, working together on the same land, and there were also strong bonds of submission through the authority the father exercised over them (Carrasco, 1993; 1982). In other words, the internal family relationships reinforced the configuration of extended family structures. These were characterised by a strong cohesion, by the maintenance of dependency relations, or by different types of control of the children by the parents and especially by the male family head, as well as by an almost inexistent freedom of action and choice. The latter showed itself, for example, in the absence of the freedom to choose one's spouse and in the common practice of arranged marriage. The relation established between structure, family relationships, and kinship relationships was very clear and corresponded to a particular type of society, in which the relation with the land was an important organizing principle. Effectively, the possibilities for an individual to survive outside this system were very limited. The individual had to accept the economic and social dependence of the male family head to survive within this society.

Several authors, among them Malvido (1982) and Gonzalbo (1998) have pointed out that from the Spanish Conquest in the 16th century and the Christianization on, the indigenous family reduced its size and developed a tendency towards nuclearization. The surge of epidemics, the establishment of debt-induced servitude (*peonaje*) with the consequent eradication of the members of the nuclear family, migration, and the spreading practice of selling the labor force were factors which fragmented the families and eroded the dependency ties that maintained this family type. However, how did this process of nuclearization manifest itself in terms of the three dimensions outlined above, and what was its meaning regarding the emergence of the modern nuclear family?

THE FIRST DIMENSION: THE FAMILY STRUCTURE DURING THE COLONIAL PERIOD

From the point of view of family structure, several studies have been elaborated on different regions of the country, which indicate a general reduction of the size of the homes in comparison with the size, of eight on average, registered at the beginning of the colonial period. This reduction presented itself especially among individuals "without sense" (*sin razón*), as the indigenous not converted to Catholicism were classified, and in the country's central regions. Borah and Sherburne (1977) have argued that the average size of the domestic units was larger in the North and in the larger villages than in the South and in the central regions. It fluctuated between approximately four and six members.

However, the size of the households varied according to not only the region of the country, but also according to the ethnic origin or the occupational status of the household head. Therefore, its size was generally bigger among individuals "of reason" (*de razón*), as the Christian Spanish were classified, and among the mixed population (*pardos,* mulattos, and black) than among the indigenous (Borah and Sherburne, 1977; Kanter, 1992). Households also tended towards being bigger if the occupational or social status of the household head was higher (Kanter, 1992; García, 1992).

The size of the households provides us with an important element for the determination of the family structure, but by itself does not inform us about its structure. The decisive variable for this definition lies in the composition of kinship, which is the kinship relationship of the household members with the household head. This means that to determine the process of nuclearization, it is necessary to consider this variable. Here, as well as in the registers regarding the size of the families, we encounter important differences. Various studies have reported the growing presence of the nuclear structure in different regions of the country towards the end of the 18th century (Robinson, 1993; Grajales, 1991; Rabell 1996; Kanter, 1992). Nevertheless, the process of nuclearization tendentially manifested itself more among the indigenous, *pardo*, and *mestizos*. Among the Spanish and the *criollos*, i.e. the children of Spanish living in the new Colony, however, the extended family structure was more common.

The previous insights allow us to formulate some clarifications. The first point is that the process of nuclearization of the family in Mexico was not a product of a process of industrialization or the development of modern institutions. Just as in the case of the European studies that refuted the thesis of nuclearization in relation to the emergence of modern society, it is clear in our case that the growing emergence and diffusion of the nuclear structure was tied to other processes, such as the progressive reduction of the population as a consequence of epidemics as well as important social transformations.

A second important aspect to be mentioned lies in the widespread idea that, following the Conquest, the Spanish implanted the occidental model of the nuclear family (Malvido, 1982). In the light of the available information, this idea has to be modified. Many authors (Gonzalbo, 1998; Grajales, 1991; Kanter, 1992) have established that as much the size as the composition of kinship relations among the Spanish and *criollo* elite were indicative of extended or complex families. Although among some indigenous, normally belonging to higher social strata, there was a tendency to adopt or 'imitate' patterns of family formation, as indicated by Gonzalbo (1998), this was not a general trend. Therefore it seems inexact to argue that the Spanish model of family formation implanted and spread in an extensive manner the model of the nuclear conjugal family in colonial society. Based on the reviewed studies, it seems evident that the Spanish arrived with a number of social and cultural patterns regarding the formation and composition of the family that they kept reproducing throughout the Colony. Among this ethnic group, the process of nuclearization was manifested in a more tenuous form. The impact of these patterns on society was limited and of differential influence on distinct social groups.

On the other hand, we have to consider a further element related to the marriage regime dominant in Spain at the time of contact with the American world. Spanish society then did not show a regime of late marriage with high rates of celibacy, a feature associated with the development of capitalist culture (Hajnal, 1965). Neither was this type of mentality characteristic of this society. In the 16th century in Andalusia, Extremadura and Castile–the origins of most of the Conquistadors, a marriage regime was dominant in which marriage was almost universal for women, the Christian ones as much as the Moors, and took place at a relatively early age between 19 and 20 years. Although besides marriage there were other patterns of consensual union, such as the *amacebamiento*, the *barragania*, the kidnapping, and the escape, the former was the normative model which the Catholic Church tried to implant. Equally, in the indigenous society in America, there was a dominant regime of marriage at an early age–at around 15 years for women and around 16 or 17 years for men (McCaa, 1996; López Austin, 1982). There were thus similarities between both societies regarding the marriage regime, but the latter was not associated with the formation of the modern conjugal nuclear family. Furthermore, in spite of these similarities, both showed differences concerning cultural patterns of family formation and internal family relationships.

One last aspect that has to be considered within the analysis of predominant types of family structure during the colonial period is that of neolocality. This is a central issue in so far as it denotes a higher level of individuation of the nuclear family structure and in so far as it constitutes an important dimension in the process of family formation. It means that the latter's structure is based on strong individualist forces, which manifest themselves in the freedom to choose one's partner, economic autonomy, in the socio-cultural assumption on the part of the couple that they have to maintain themselves on their own economically–all of which expresses itself in the formation of a new household separate from the families of origin at the time of the union.

This point has rarely been treated in the literature, but there are indicators that neolocality presented itself in a partial way and not as an important pattern in the structuring of the family units. For the Spanish, there are few data describing to what extent and with which depth neolocality was present, and the tendency rather seems to have been to form extensive and large structures. On the part of the indigenous groups, the literature has described the way in which young couples recently united or married went to the home of the bridegroom's father to live there for some time before forming their own household. This means that the patrilocality described as a valid pattern since the period prior to the Conquest continued to present itself during colonial times. Therefore, although nuclearisation of the family structure took place among indigenous groups, from the socio-cultural point of view and in terms of the internal family relationships, this pattern was not adopted.

THE SECOND DIMENSION: FAMILY RELATIONSHIPS DURING THE COLONIAL PERIOD

As already pointed out, the patterns characteristic of the model of family formation in Spain during the 16th century did not constitute an explanatory factor for the growing presence of the nuclear family structure in New Spain, as Mexico was called during the Spanish colonial rule. Rather, explanations have to be sought in the social processes and the reduction of the population that took place during the first two centuries of the Colony era. However, a further factor has to be added, which has a great cultural impact and played a decisive role in the transformation of family relationships: the Christianization and the role of the Catholic Church. They made the most significant contribution towards a modern configuration of family relationships.

The new laws regarding engagement and marriage established at the Council of Trent had significant effects on the respective models in New Spain. To specify these effects, we need to analyze what were the rites of engagement and marriage practiced in the Spanish colonies and in Catholic Europe. Lavrin (1991) argues that the word "*casamiento*" (marriage, wedding) was key to initiating regular or irregular relationships among the men and women of the Colony. The word "*casamiento*" as a binding contract between individuals was a medieval Spanish ritual, which appears described in the Spanish laws of the "*Siete Partidas*". They summarize the different interpretations of this ritual by the Canonists Graciano and Lombardo in the 12th century. The Church unified the positions of both theologists in 1179, when Pope Alexander III, accepted the promise of future marriage as a union not yet realized. If there was a sexual encounter prior to the marriage ceremony, with or without an intervention on the part of the Church, the union had been consummated and was valid. Verbal promises could be revoked in the case that there had been no sexual encounter. In this understanding, therefore, the physical union played a central role. In the *Siete Partidas*, furthermore, authority was given to the bishops to oblige those who had dissolved a commitment to honor their word if it had been given with the agreement of both parties, even if there had been no witnesses (Lavrin, 1991: 17-18).

According to Lavrin (1991), the Council of Trent took the final step in the regulation of marriage by establishing a definite marriage ritual, which required witnesses and a priest to hold the ceremony. This conceptualization of the word "*casamiento*" and the regulations of marriage had important consequences in New Spain, in so far as there was a diffusion of some of the characteristics of the Spanish Continental ceremony and, above all, its basic intention to lend legitimacy to the commitment as initiation of the marriage (Lavrin, 1991: 18-19).

Effectively, the institution of Catholic marriage under this conceptualization was a process that frequently had contrary effects, i.e., the spreading of illegitimate unions. Under the promise of marriage, backed by the Church, the practices of seduction, *concubinato*, and *amacebamiento* found fertile ground. This point is supported by an analysis of the claims presented in ecclesiastical tribunals concerning failings to honor promises of marriage (Seed, 1994; Pescador, 1994). The Church's intention to instate Catholic marriage in this sense had paradoxical effects. The promise of marriage contributed to the emergence of an emotional dynamic in the practice of courtship, which furthered the spreading of consensual or informal unions, the covering-up of polygamy and bigamy, and, consequently, the generation of the highest rates of illegitimacy registered during the Colony. These phenomena presented themselves more is the Hispanicized and urban regions that in the rural and indigenous ones, where the rates of illegitimacy were much lower (McCaa, 1996; Pescador, 1992).

Another issue regarding the Catholic regulation of marriage with important consequences was the weight given to consensuality. Whether marriage had to be an expression of the will of the couple or whether it had to be followed from the will or interests of the parents and the family was something strongly debated since the Middle Ages and which continues to be an important point in New Spain. The theologist Graciano established the principle of consensuality and free will concerning marriage and declared it void in the case of any type of coercion. The couple was free to agree and realize marriage by means of the joint promise and/or the following sexual union. The Council of Trent did not modify the idea of the necessity of consensuality, which remained as one of the cornerstones of Christian marriage in the Catholic Church (Lavrin 1991). Nevertheless, defending the freedom of spousal choice, the Church practically encouraged the diffusion of seduction, kidnapping, and escape. Equally, this introduced important patterns of individualization by weakening the position of community and family interests regarding the formation of unions. Thus, while the Church generated individualizing patterns, the civil laws kept recognizing the interests of family and state, giving greater power to the parents in the establishment of marriage. Later on, the reforms to Spanish law in 1776 and 1803 were directed at a strengthening of parental control over marriage, requiring written parental permission for the promises of marriage of young people under age to be of legal value; but they also strengthened the power of man in courtship and in the marriage agreement. This took place, depriving women of their rights to present claims based on the breaking of promises and seduction. With these reforms, the support for choices based on the involved individuals' free will given by the Church was effectively marginalized (Lavrin, 1991; McCaa, 1996).

These aspects of the regulation of marriage showed effects mostly among the Spanish, *criollo*, and *mestizo* population, as well as in the most urbanized zones. In contrast, among the indigenous, the influence of the Catholic Church on the formation of family relations, specifically regarding unions and marriage, had other effects. One that deserves special attention is the prohibition of polygamy, which mostly affected the indigenous nobility, and of marriage among kin in the first or second degree. These rules consequently abolished the *levirato*, an important custom within which the widow with her children came to be an additional wife of the brother of her late husband (Carrasco, 1975). This had an effect on the traditional forms in which unions were formed which followed a more complex and wide kinship pattern than the one contemplated in Christian marriage. Equally, the defense of free will in the choice of a spouse contravened the custom according to which the family and the community intervened in the process of family formation. The most important result of these measures – from my point of view – was the initiation of a process leading towards the limitation of the wider kinship ties and of community ties in the formation of families and a tendency towards the formation of more restricted family groups which enjoyed a greater autonomy with regard to kinship and community networks. In summary, these measures pointed towards a higher degree of individualization not only on the part of the individuals–in terms of freedom of spousal choice–but also regarding the family core with regard to kinship networks.

Gruzinski (1991) has indicated that Catholicism as value system was a factor which promoted a certain level of secularization by espousing a vision of the person grounded in his or her free will, whose destiny depended on his or her own acts and not on supernatural forces. In this system, the indigenous was isolated from the system of supernatural forces and of traditional social ties surrounding her or him: destiny, the intervention or anger of a God, the practices of a witch, the envy of a neighbor all ceased to be factors explaining individual conduct. The latter found himself or herself alone before God and was responsible for her or his own acts.

It seems difficult to evaluate to which extent the indigenous adopted in a profound way an individualist conceptualization of the individual, and we cannot establish with precision the impact, which these individualizing tendencies had. The studies realized until now seem to agree on the indigenous adopting them in some ways but in others in partial and superficial way or with resistance and on them seeking ways to preserve many of their practices and beliefs (Gonzalbo, 1998).

The rise of Christian marriage confronted strong resistance among the leading or noble class, among which polygamy was common. Among the *macehuales* (common people, indigenous peasants), in contrast, it spread more rapidly, but also in a more superficial way, in the form of apparent submission to imposed principles. Given that among them monogamous unions were common, their regularization by means of the execution of the Christian rite did not mean an abandoning of their practices. The indigenous effectively married in Church without the adoption of this behavior implying a profound acceptance of the Christian understanding–much rather it implied the latter's manipulation in order to adapt it to their own principles (Legros, 1982; Gonzalbo, 1998). Thus–as Gruzinski indicates–they did not understand, for example, the marital rites and supposed that marriage was not an expression of mutual agreement and a commitment, but rather the reception of a blessing on the occasion of marriage. In general, the most important moment for them was not the religious ceremony but rather the moment of commitment (Gruzinski, 1991: 120).

Christian marriage therefore introduced individualizing patterns but did not manage to uproot the native customs and understandings. Still at the end of the Colonial period and still during the 20th century an idiosyncratic family behavior was dominant in rural communities, in which paternal authority was imposed, the families intervened in spousal selection, and kinship loyalties were respected (Pescador, 1992). Equally, patrilocality persisted as pattern of family formation, because of which neolocality in a social and cultural sense, as mentioned above, only presented itself in a partial manner. This patrilocality revealed the persistence of more traditional forms of family structuring.

Gruzinski (1991) has indicated that this new understanding of marriage fomented conjugal intimacy, intensified spiritual and affective communion among the spouses, tended to establish reciprocity and parity regarding sexual exchanges within marriage, and promoted obligations between parents and children. This hypothesis has very important conceptual consequences, which have to be explained and ordered. It assumes that the mentioned understanding ties the configuration of a type of nuclear family to certain characteristics at the level of emotions and bonds among the couple and between them and their children. The formation of a space in which affectivity and intimacy are concentrated and in which there are egalitarian relationships has effectively been identified as one of the typical features of the modern nuclear family (Stone, 1983; Parsons & Bales, 1955). The affectivity previously spread among different kin, the obligations–including those of an affective nature–towards parents and the community, and the submission to them was thus concentrated in the new nucleus: in the couple and their children. The care for and the obligations towards the latter occupied a central and privileged place, those towards kin and community being remitted to secondary importance without disappearing completely. Nevertheless, in Colonial society the individualizing tendencies had very specific limits. In the existing studies until now there are no indicators of the indigenous, the Spanish, or other socio-ethnic groups holding a firm understanding of individual liberty and of the privileged position of the individual dimension of social life over the group-based and collective ones. In this society, communitarian understandings were dominant, although it is equally true that the individual dimension acquired greater space and autonomy.

Equally, the above mentioned hypothesis maintains that the said understanding of marriage favored the formation of more egalitarian relationships among the sexes –a point which has to be refuted based on evidence which shows that relationships in fact were profoundly unequal and that men were allocated a superior and prioritized position. Furthermore, the configuration of the nuclear family as space in which intimacy, sexuality, and affectivity were concentrated should be taken with caution, given the presence of other types of union, such as the *amancebamiento*. It should equally be considered that the religious bond had not been instituted as a space for expression of self and the exercise of eroticism and sexuality in a wider sense, but rather for the purposes of procreation and education of the children. In this sense, conjugal love may be considered as a secondary, if not dangerous, feeling for the proper functioning of the conjugal relationship, given that respect and obedience were of greater importance. Sexual desire among the couple was seen as clearly deleterious for Catholic marital life and as one of the 'best' opportunities the spouses had for loosing their souls. For this reason, the conjugal obligations (*débito conyugal*) formed the only space to which sexuality was restricted (Pescador, 1988). Although the Church attempted to foment the formation of a space for intimacy and affects within the family, this happened very slowly and not until the 19th century during the Victorian period, when it assumed an important role.

From a socio-cultural viewpoint, thus, during the Colonial period no development of family relationships of the type corresponding to the nuclear family in the aforementioned sense took place. Nevertheless, we may say that the regulation of marriage and its implementation tended towards demarcating a familial space through which kinship relationships were tied to the family nucleus. By emphasizing the relationship among the couple and between the couple and their children, said conceptualization opposed the polygamic tendencies and the formation of lineages, but internally it led to relationships that were unequal, hierarchical, and characterized by a low level of individualization. In this sense, the family only nuclearized or individualized itself with regard to its kinship network: It nuclearized itself in relation to its exterior, but internally it did not show relationships of a modern type.

Asymmetry and inequality characterized the relationships among the couple and between it and its children. This point can be supported with the observation that both in the Christian understanding and in the civil one marriage was based on a patriarchal system which manifested itself in the exercise of the *patria potestad* (legal authority or custody) by men. The *patria potestad* attributed certain authority rights to men regarding their dealings with women and denied the latter the right to manage their property, to choose their own residence, or to assume some responsibility of their own lives. Men had the right to call women to order, and women and children had to submit themselves to their authority. They therefore expected total obedience on the part of their wives and children, and in return they provided maintenance, protection and guidance. Another example of the profound inequalities and the authoritarianism within family relationships lies in the regulation in Spanish law applied in New Spain regarding wife killings (uxoricide) and cases of domestic violence to be treated in tribunals (Pescador, 1996; Lipsett-Rivera, 1996).

Analyzing the relationships among parents and children, we can observe that they did not conform family relationships corresponding to the type of the nuclear modern family. They were in fact not only characterized by asymmetric relations through the exercise of the *patria potestad* as indicated above, but also the space and the meaning of childhood was much more limited. Civil and canonic legislation closed the doors of childhood and opened those of adulthood with the possibility of marriage between 12 and 14 years for women and men respectively. Puberty was a very weak notion previous to the end of the 19th century, when the idea of childhood was widened considerably in the context of the introduction of state-led education (Lavrin, 1991). The Church attempted to foment the duties of care towards the children, but this was taken up in a differential way within different socio-ethnic groups. Therefore, in some cities, such as Antequera–today Oaxaca–and likely in other urban zones as well, the following tendency showed itself: the children of the Spanish continued to be children of their families until they came of age, at which point they had to leave their homes; in contrast, the children of the indigenous had to leave their homes at a very early age–at around ten years. This early abandonment is in part to be attributed to the practice widespread among the indigenous to send their children to other households to learn some office, as documented by Rabell (1996).

CONCLUDING REMARKS

The historical analysis of the three dimensions of the family, i.e., its structure, its internal relationships, and the kinship relationships, helps illustrate that the nuclear family structure was a reality that formed in important ways since the colonial period, above all among the indigenous population. However, in spite of this pattern of nuclearization, changes at the level of family relationships showed a much slower pace in the concretization of modern features. Therefore we may conclude that family relationships acquired some characteristics of the nuclear family in the sense that they tended towards greater closeness, individualization, and the weakening of wider kinship ties. In terms of the three family types identified by Stone (1983), i.e. the "family with open lineage", the "restricted nuclear patriarchal family", and the "closed domestic nuclear family", we may conclude that within the prehispanic period the first family type tended to be dominant.

During the Colonial period this family type still presented itself in important ways both among the Spanish and the indigenous. Equally, it is likely that in both ethnic groups conjugal and kinship relationships were more distant in the sense that affectivity developed in a diffused way with regard to a wide kinship network. In this family type, as explained by Stone (1983), there was no sense of domestic intimacy; the interpersonal relationships within the family were rather distant, in part due to high mortality rates which made death a concrete possibility and impeded affective involvement and in part due to cultural models requiring arranged marriages, the agreement of dowry, the subordination of women, and the custom to entrust one's children at an early age to strangers. Therefore, while among the indigenous nuclear structures and relationships of the "family with open lineage" could be found, among the Spanish there were both extended structures and family relationships of the "open lineage" type.

Also, during the colonial period from a socio-cultural standpoint, another type of family relationships emerged that is closer to the second type of family– the "restricted nuclear patriarchal family"–identified by Stone (1983). This type of family relationships that began to develop was characterized by a reduction of the importance of kinship and community and by a growing weight of the conjugal union–fundamentally favored by the Catholic Church–and of patriarchy. This growing individuation of the family nucleus took place with the spreading of the promise of marriage as mechanism for legitimizing marital and conjugal relationships. This favored the emergence of not only the freedom of spousal choice but also of the generation of a space-marriage–in which sexuality and affection united and expressed themselves and grew, supplanting economic interests. On the other hand, the Church insisted in the differences emanating from the hierarchical order and the necessity to reproduce in the family the divine order, which was unequal and authoritarian. This promoted the dominance of the interests of the group or the patriarch over individual ones. This collectivist tendency was reinforced by the rules established in Spanish law regarding the position of parents in agreement of marriage. This family type was formed more among the Spanish than among the indigenous, and more in urban than in rural areas.

In the type of the "restricted nuclear patriarchal family" developed by Stone, family relationships were shaped by Protestantism, which fomented individualism; however, in difference from the English case, in New Spain Catholicism was spread, which fortified family-centered patterns and only to a lesser degree individualist tendencies. Apart from the continuing influence of parents and the families of origin in the agreement of marriage, the authoritarianism defining the intrafamilial relationships, i.e. the duties of children and wife towards father and husband, denoted a very important value orientation giving force to familism. This explains how at the same time that family relationships individualized or nuclearized themselves with regard to kinship and community, their internal cohesion was reinforced, leaving individualisms as such with only a very limited space. Catholic morality furthermore served as an element fortifying internal cohesion.

These tendencies continued throughout the Colony and beyond until the mid-19th century. It is until this moment that the nuclear conjugal family begins to emerge, above all among the Spanish and *mestizo* population. From the socio-cultural point of view, at the level of family relationships, some of the features of the third family type indicated by Stone–the "closed nuclear domestic family"– began to emerge within the process of secularization that initiated towards the middle of this century. It manifested itself in the separation of Church and state, the formation of civil legislation, the founding of schools as spaces specifically dedicated to the education of children, and the institution of marriage as a civil contract established based on the liberty of choice of the involved individuals (Staples, 1999; Ramos, in press). These phenomena produced a clearer separation of the conjugal nucleus and above all the formation of the family as a space in which domesticity, intimacy, romantic love, the cultivation of childhood and the understanding of the family as an affect-based space (Zermeño, 1996). It was in this moment that the definition of modern gender roles was established in a precise way, although they were profoundly unequal, permeated by Catholic morality and based on a strong biologist understanding of gender differences. Women directed their attention towards childcare, their husbands, and the development of a private role, while the husbands, in contrast, defined for themselves a public role as providers and agents in charge of the family groups' social mobility (Speckman, 2002). It was equally until this moment that the freedom of spousal choice, promoted for such a long time by the Catholic Church against Spanish law, broke free of its constraints and became widespread and firmly rooted, due to the new republican civil legislation which abolished the possibility of interference by the families of origin in marital arrangements. From this point on, financial considerations or familial economic interests in the agreement of a dowry and marital arrangements were less decisive, and, in turn, the prospect of future personal happiness based in consolidated affects became more important (Zermeño, 1996). To some extent, from the middle of that century on, the development began of what Stone (1983) labeled "affective individualism". Nevertheless, in difference from the English case, in which the latter promoted a tendency towards gender equality, in independent Mexico its diffusion also encountered limits, in so far as patriarchy and strong gender inequality persisted, and in so far as the development of eroticism within marriage faced strong barriers within the Victorian culture dominant at the time.

This formative process of the nuclear family reveals that each of the dimensions noted (structure, family relationships, kinship relationships) followed a distinct course. This means that during the Colonial period the nuclear structure was spread, but that the formation of modern family relationships of the nuclear type did not take place until the middle of the 19th century. At this moment, family structure and family relationships converged in a specific family form, which gradually spread through other sectors of Mexican society. Kinship relationships, furthermore, were more clearly differentiated from the familial nucleus. However, this family type did not spread to all sectors of society, and it is for this reason that even now we can observe more traditional modes of organization, especially in rural areas and among indigenous groups.

REFERENCES

To Rene, an intimate presence.

Ariés, P. (1987). El niño y la vida familiar en el Antiguo Régimen. Madrid: Taurus.

Barbagli, M. (1987). Strutture e relazioni familiari. In Tranfaglia N. & Firpo M. (Eds.), La Storia, (pp. 23-43). Turín: UTET.

Borah, W., and Sherburne, F. C. (1977). Ensayos sobre historia de la población: México y el Caribe. México: Siglo XXI Editores.

Carrasco, P. (1993). La familia conjunta en el México antiguo: el caso de Molotla. In Gonzalbo P. (Ed.), Historia de la familia, (pp. 106-125). México: Instituto Mora/Universidad Autónoma Metropolitana.

Carrasco, P. (1982). Estructura familiar en Tepoztlán en el siglo XVI. Nueva Antropología, *5* (18), 127-154.

Carrasco, P. (1975). La transformación de la cultura indígena durante la colonia. Historia mexicana, 25(2), 175-203.

Durkheim, E. (1975). Introduction á la Sociologie de la Famille. Paris: Les Editions de Minuit.

García, F. (1992). Los muros de la vida privada y la familia: Casa y tamaño familar en Zacatecas. Primeras décadas del siglo XIX. Estudios Demográficos y Urbanos, 7(1), 35-52.

Gonzalbo, P. (1998). Familia y orden colonial. México: El Colegio de México.

Grajales, A. (1991). Hogares de la villa de Atlixco a fines de la colonia: estados, calidades y ejercicios de sus Cabezas, in Gonzalbo P. (Ed.), Familias novohispanas, Siglos XVI al XIX, (pp. 325-342). México: El Colegio de México.

Gruzinski, S. (1991). Individualización y aculturación: la confesión entre los nahuas de México entre los siglos XVI y XVII. In Lavrin, A. (Ed.) Sexualidad y matrimonio en la América hispánica. Siglos XVI-XVIII, (pp. 105-126). México: Consejo Nacional para la Cultura y las Artes/ Grijalbo.

Hajnal, J. (1965). European Marriage Patterns in Perspective. In D. Glass & E. Eversley (Eds.) Population in History: Essays in Historical Demography, (pp. 101-143). London: Edward Arnold Publisher.

INEGI (Instituto Nacional de Estadística, Geografía e Informática). (2003). Population Census. México City: Instituto Nacional de Estadística, Geografía e Informática.

Kanter, D. (1992). Viudas y vecinos, milpas y magueyes. El impacto del auge de la población en el Valle de Toluca: el caso de Tenango del Valle en el siglo XVII. Estudios Demográficos y Urbanos, 7(1), 19-33.

König, R. (1970). Old Problems and New Queries in Family Sociology. In König R. & Hill R. (Eds.), Families in East and West. Paris: Mouton.

Laslett, P. (Ed.) (1972). Household and Family in Past Time. Cambridge: University of Cambridge Press.

Lavrín, A. (1991). Introducción: el escenario, los actores y el problema. In Lavrín, A. (Ed.), Sexualidad y matrimonio en la América hispánica. Siglos XVI-XVII, (pp. 13-52). México: Consejo Nacional para la Cultura y las Artes/Grijalbo.

Legros, M. (1982). Acerca de un diálogo que no lo fue. In Burguiére A., Revel J., Giraud F., Malvido E., Ortega S., Boyer R., López Austin A., et. al. Familia y sexualidad en Nueva España, (pp. 207-237). México: SEP/80/Fondo de Cultura Económica.

Lévi-Strauss, C. (1995). La familia. In C. Lévi-Strauss, M. Spiro & K. Gough (Eds.) Polémica sobre el origen y universalidad de la familia. Barcelona: Anagrama.

Lipsett-Rivera, S. (1996). La violencia dentro de las familias formal e informal. In Gonzalbo P. & Rabell C. (Eds.) Familia y vida privada en la historia de Iberoamérica, (pp. 325-340). México: El Colegio de México/ Universidad Nacional Autónoma de México.

Litwak, Eugene (1960a). Occupational Mobility and Extended Family Cohesion. *American Sociological Review,* 25 (1): 82-109.

Litwak, Eugene (1960b). Geographic Mobility and Extended Family Cohesion. *American Sociological Review,* 25 (3): 153-171.

López Austin, A. (1982). La sexualidad entre los antiguos nahuas. In Burguiére A., Revel J., Giraud F., Malvido E., Ortega S., Boyer R., López Austin A., et. al. Familia y sexualidad en Nueva España, (pp. 141-176). México: SEP/80/Fondo de Cultura Económica.

Malvido, E. (1982). Algunos aportes de los estudios de demografía histórica al estudio de la familia en la época colonial de México. In Burguiére A., Revel J., Giraud F., Malvido E., Ortega S., Boyer R., López Austin A., et. al. Familia y sexualidad en Nueva España, (pp. 81-99). México: Fondo de Cultura Económica/SEP/80.

McCaa, R. (1996). Tratos nupciales: la constitución de uniones formales e informales en México y España, 1500-1900. In Gonzalbo P. & Rabell C. (Eds.), Familia y vida privada en la historia de Iberoamérica, (pp. 21-57). México: El Colegio de México, UNAM.

McLaughlin, V. (1971). Patterns of Work and Family Organization: Buffalo´s Italians. *Journal of Interdisciplinary History,* 2 (2), 299-314.

Parsons, T. (1980) Respuesta a sus críticos. In Anderson M. (Ed.) Sociología de la familia, (pp. 114-115). México: Fondo de Cultura Económica.

Parsons, T. & Robert Bales (Eds.) (1955). Family, Socialization and Interaction Process. Glencoe: The Free Press.

Pescador, J. (1996). Del dicho al hecho: uxoricidios en el México central, 1769-1820. In Gonzalbo P. & Rabell C. (Eds.) Familia y vida privada en la historia de Iberoamérica, (pp. 373-386). México: El Colegio de México/Universidad Nacional Autónoma de México.

Pescador, J. (1994). Entre la espada y el olvido: pleitos matrimoniales en el provisorato eclesiástico de México, siglo XVIII. In P. Pilar & C. Rabell (Eds.) La familia en el mundo iberoamericano, (pp. 193-226). México: Instituto de Investigaciones Sociales-Universidad Nacional Autónoma de México.

Pescador, J. (1992). La nupcialidad urbana preindustrial y los límites del mestizaje: características y evolución de los patrones de nupcialidad en la Ciudad de México, 1700-1850, in Estudios Demográficos y Urbanos, 7(1), 137-168.

Pescador, J. (1988) Confesores y casaderas: la nupcialidad subyacente en la ética matrimonial de la iglesia novohispana. Estudios demográficos y urbanos, 3(2), 291-324.

Rabell, C. (1996). Trayectoria de vida familiar, raza y género en Oaxaca colonial. In Gonzalbo P. & Rabell C. (Eds.) Familia y vida privada en la historia de Iberoamérica, (pp. 75-118). México: El Colegio de México/ Universidad Nacional Autónoma de México.

Ramos, C. (in press). Cambio jurídico y jerarquía familiar en el México decimonónico. In Barros M. & Esteinou R. (Eds.) Análisis del cambio sociocultural. México: Centro de Investigaciones y Estudios Superiores en Antropología Social.

Robinson, D. (1993). Patrones de población: Parral a fines del siglo XVIII. In Malvido E. & Cuenya M. A. (Eds.) Demografía histórica de México. Siglos XVI-XIX, (pp. 179-216) México: Instituto Mora/Universidad Autónoma Metropolitana.

Seed, Patricia (1994). La narrativa del Don Juan: el lenguaje de la seducción en la literatura y la sociedad hispánicas del siglo XVII In P. Gonzalbo & C. Rabell (Eds.) La familia en el mundo iberoamericano, (pp. 91-125). México: Instituto de Investigaciones Sociales-UNAM.

Sennett, R. (1984). Families Against the City. Cambridge, Massachusetts: Harvard University Press.

Shorter, E. (1975). The Making of the Modern Family. New York: Basic Books.

Speckman, E. (2002). Crimen y castigo. México: El Colegio de México/ Universidad Nacional Autónoma de México.

Staples, Anne (1999). La transición hacia una moral laica. In Gonzalbo P. (Ed.) Familia y educación en Iberoamérica, (pp. 139-152). México: El Colegio de México.

Stone, L. (1983). Famiglia, sesso e matrimonio in Inghilterra. Tra cinque e ottocento. Turín: Einaudi.

Zermeño, G. (1996). La retórica del amor romántico: familia y matrimonio en León, 1884-1907. In Gonzalbo P. & Rabell C. (Eds.) Familia y vida privada en la historia de Iberoamérica, (pp. 489-506). México: El Colegio de México/Universidad Nacional Autónoma de México.

STATE PRAGMATISM VERSUS IDEOLOGY: FAMILY PLANNING IN THE ISLAMIC REPUBLIC OF IRAN

7

Akbar Aghajanian & Amir H. Mehryar

INTRODUCTION

State intervention in the Iranian family domain started in the first quarter of the 20th century when Reza Khan came to power and made himself the Shah of Iran and the constitutional monarch (Lapidus, 1988:580-581). As part of his modernization effort, Reza Shah reorganized the judicial administration, which was traditionally under the jurisdiction of Islamic religious leadership. New civil law codes were introduced in 1928 which replaced the *Shari' a* and the registration of all legal documents was turned over to secular courts and government branches dealing with different affairs. Historically most family affair matters were handled within the tradition of religion and local norms and practices. Marriage and divorce were witnessed by local religious leaders and recorded on the back of the family Quran. The new law required the registration of all marriages and divorces in notary offices and quarterly reporting of all these events to the secular judicial system. The law also required the registration of birth and death in the civil registration organization. For the first time, a legal age of marriage for women and men were introduced and penalties were defined for deviance from the civil law (Momeni, 1972). Despite continuing expansion of intervention of state into family and family affairs as state led modernization continued in the first half of the 20th century, interference in family size and effort to influence the number of birth did not come until 1960s.

Serious state interference with family size and birth control in Iran started in 1967 with the adoption of a national family planning policy. Faced with challenges of a fast growing population and the constraints on economic growth, after some flirtation with a pronatalist policy, the Imperial Government of Iran adopted a national family planning program in 1967. At the time Iran and Turkey constituted the largest non-Arabic speaking Muslim population of the Middle East. Surrounded by the ideologically challenging Soviet Union on the North and the often hostile Arab Nationalism on the South, imperial Iran had every reason to aim at a larger and rapidly growing population both to protect it against its rapidly growing Arab neighbors and to support the creation of the regional power that the Shah had long aspired for. Thus the government's hesitation in signing the first UN resolution on the responsibility of national governments for controlling the growth of their population in early 1960s was less surprising than its decision to adopt a birth control policy and launched a serious national family planning program a few years later.

The population and family planning program of Iran was launched in an environment that could hardly be regarded as favorable for its survival and success. The general intellectual climate of the country, like many other developing countries of the decade, was not convinced of either the dire impact of rapid population growth on socioeconomic development or the inability of a vast and oil rich country like Iran to accommodate a much larger population than the figure of 26 million revealed by the 1966 census. Moreover, the majority of the population, particularly those living in rural areas, were illiterate and highly tradition bound. Infant mortality was high and due to the absence of a social security system most parents regarded high fertility not only of religious value but also as insurance against potential loss of children and old age poverty. Having multiple children, particularly boys, was not only a source of pride and prestige but also economic security for most Iranian women who could be easily divorced if they were unable to produce a son (Behnam, 1961). Having early and universal marriage encouraged by both Islamic traditions and the national culture of Iran was considered a major and almost unbeatable obstacle to fertility decline (Momeni, 1972). Under the circumstances, a low profile family planning program might have had a better chance of success. Instead, the leadership of the program began with a good deal of publicity and paid relatively little attention to existing political and religious sensitivities. They showed much more interest in building tactical political alliances with the then prevalent sources of political power than establishing strategic links with religious leaders and low profile political and professional organizations and community leaders that might have provided them with long-term public credibility and support.

In late 1960s Imperial Iran was regarded as one of the most important, rapidly modernizing, and dependable allies of the United States in the Middle East region and every effort was made to turn it into a show case of Western style development strategies and to use its military might for dealing with regional trouble makers. Thus, a host of advisers from the Population Council and US universities active in the area of population and family planning were sent in to help the Iranian government with the implementation of a family planning program. On the other hand as an indication of the insensitivity of the program to the traditional values of Iranian society, it may be worth noting that no official effort was made to obtain a formal religious ruling (*fatwa*) in support of contraception and family planning from any of the top level religious leaders then reigning in the Iranian theological centers in the cities of Qum and Mashad.

Despite its forceful effort to influence family size through increasing the adoption of family planning and birth control, this state sponsored program did not have a significant effect throughout its duration from 1967-1979 when it was dismantled by the Islamic Revolutionary government. A large amount of the country's resources were allocated to the family planning program and aggressive publicity and social marketing activities were undertaken in early 1970s. But the achievements of the program on influencing family size were modest. Official statistics supplied to the Population Council for 1978, the last year before the Revolution, gave the estimated number of contraceptive users from all sources as 1,358,000 (Nortman and Hofstatter, 1979). The Iran Fertility Survey (IFS, 1977), the last and probably the most reliable source of information on the performance of the Iranian family planning program shortly before its suspension (Statistical Center of Iran, 1986; Aghajanian *et al.,* 1995), gave a 37 per cent contraceptive prevalence rate. This is of course mainly due to the inclusion of a large proportion of women who reported using the non-program dependent traditional method of withdrawal. The rates of current contraceptive use were however much lower for the rural (20 per cent) and illiterate (25 per cent) couples, those aged below 20 years (16.5 per cent), and those with lower parities (31 per cent). Among rural women with 3 or fewer children, only 10 per cent were using a contraceptive. In the end this huge state intervention effort only resulted in a slight change in family size—measured by a total fertility rate of 7.0 in 1966 to a rate of 6.3 in 1976.

A NEW STATE IDEOLOGY AND FAMILY PLANNING

When the Islamic Revolution erupted suddenly in mid-1978, the family planning program could count on few friends among the lay and religious groups involved in the Revolution. Moreover, both the rank and file personnel running the program and the public interested in using its services were uncertain as to the place of contraception and family planning in the new array of values and virtues ushered in by the Revolution. The Iranian Revolution of 1979 was a truly nationwide phenomenon that had attracted the participation of the overwhelming majority of the population. Individuals and groups with quite contrasting characteristics, beliefs, and expectations had taken part in it. Hence, ideologies were many and were the guiding light for action and behavior regarding any policy including the state sponsored family planning program and state desire to influence family size. The Temporary Revolutionary government believed that underdevelopment and dependency on the Western imperialist world order was the main problem facing Iran. They further thought that Iran had the necessary resources and manpower to embark on rapid development and modernization. The first elected president, the French trained Bani-Sadr believed that development was the best method of family planning. To the triumphant religious government, family planning was like any other sign of influence of the West and did not have any value. Hence, the program was suspended immediately after the victory of the Revolution in early 1979.

There is no doubt that the family planning program, like most other modernization efforts initiated by the Shah's regime, was viewed with suspicion by the majority of political groups involved in the Revolution. Most of them did not believe in population growth as a serious problem for an oil rich country like Iran. Many of them also considered the whole birth control movement as an American inspired plan to keep the population of Iran and other developing countries down. The close link between the family planning program and the Iranian Women's Organization headed by the Shah's powerful but highly unpopular sister, Ashraf Pahlavi, had further damaged the program. The dominant ideology did not favor any positive position of professional personnel involved in the day-to-day administration of the program. In fact, some service providers and users who were not familiar with traditional Islamic views on contraception may have had serious doubts regarding the religious permissibility of contraceptive distribution and use. Hence it was quietly let go of.

The indifference intensified as the Iraq-Iran imposed war continued and the atmosphere of war and war casualties overshadowed any state concern over the population issue and family size. In fact, the continuation of war reinforced the ideology of pronatalism implicitly and explicitly. Probably the period between 1979 and 1988, could be described as an eras of strong ideology of hands-off any state desire and intervention in family size manipulation. This did not mean the total discontinuation of family planning services and supplies either by the public or the private health sector. In fact, despite the abolition of the program and activities, the provision of services by the Mother and Child Health facilities run by the Ministry of Health (MOH, renamed as Ministry of Health and Medical Education, MOHME, since 1986) and the private health clinics and practitioners continued at a modest scale. Yet as an indication of how ideology was dominant regarding the issue of family size and population control in the first 8 years of the post-revolution, the first five year socio-economic plan of Iran did not mention any thing about population as factor in economic planning.

PRAGMATISM AND A NEW STATE FAMILY PLANNG POLICY

Starting in 1956, Iran has continued to take a national census every 10 years. The results of 1986 census indicated that almost within the first 7 years of the post- revolutionary era the population of Iran has increased roughly 11.2 million (about almost 28 per cent of the population in 1976). Specifically within the 10 years between 1976 and 1986, the population had increased with an average growth rate of 3.4 per year (Aghajanian, 1991). As the detailed results of the census became available and the leadership of the Islamic Republic realized their immediate and long-term implications for the war-shattered economy of Iran, the situation changed from one of public euphoria to private concern. This was not unexpected in view of the fact that by this time the country had depleted almost all of the foreign exchange reserves it had inherited from the old regime and, due to intensified Iraqi air attacks on oil installations and tankers, her capacity for oil production and export had been seriously curtailed. Other sectors of the economy and the industrial infrastructure built during the preceding three decades had also suffered enormously due to continuous Iraqi air attacks and loss of access to spare parts caused by the American imposed embargo. The Plan & Budget Organization (PBO), the main government agency responsible for the overall monitoring of government revenues, expenditures, development efforts, and allocation of national resources, was well aware of the vulnerable state of the economy and its inability to bear the burden of a rapidly rising, young population.

This evidence, which was later published (PBO, 1989), went a long way in alerting the leadership of the country to the dwindling resources of the nation and their insufficiency to meet the high cost of war as well as to provide the variety of social and welfare services envisioned by the Constitution. Ministers responsible for such basic services as the agriculture and food production, health, and education as well as the technical staff of the Plan and Budget Organization took every opportunity to call attention to the inevitably grave consequences of unchecked population growth and to emphasize the need for a population and birth control policy. Hence, within just a few years after the publication of the results of the 1986 census and as the Iran-Iraq hostilities was ending, ideology gave way to pragmatism and interest in a state sponsored effort to influence family size and there by to decrease the rate of population growth, intensified. In February 1988, Prime Minister Moosavi sent a secret circular to all ministries and government departments asking them to carefully consider the impact and implications of the high rate of population growth revealed by the 1986 census. Then in March 1988 a committee was organized in the Ministry of Plan and Budget, consisting mostly of the technical staff of that ministry and a few academic demographers, to prepare for organization of a population seminar. To facilitate the work of the conference committee, the Prime Minister issued a memorandum to all government ministries declaring that the government was *"reconsidering the issue of population growth"*. A highly publicized three-day "Population and Development Seminar" was held in Mashad city in September 1988. It was opened with a special message from the Prime Minister. The Ministers of Plan and Budget and Health presented detailed analyses of the implications of unchecked population growth for the socioeconomic development of the country as well as the health and welfare of its citizens. Academic demographers as well as experts from such ministries as agriculture, education, economy, and health used the opportunity to stress the need for planning and control of the population and other resources of the nation.

The resolution approved at the end of the seminar made a number of specific recommendations regarding the need for and means of population control and family planning. The seminar in effect publicly declared that the rate of population growth in Iran was too high and that, if left unchecked, it will have seriously negative effects on the national economy and the welfare of the people. The participants strongly urged the government to include population issues in policy making. At the end of the Mashad Seminar, the Minister of Health and Medical Education reiterated the late Imam Khomeini's *fatwa* regarding family planning in a press conference, and announced that a family planning program would be established. Almost simultaneously, the Prime Minister went out of his way to declare that *"birth control"* was a *"destiny factor"* for Iran and invited women to prevent unwanted pregnancies by seeking help from publicly run health clinics and health houses around the country. Within one year, by 1989, the foundation for a new state policy was established to influence the number of children families have as way to control the birth rate and population growth. This pragmatic policy was even approved by the then newly established *"Expediency Council to Safeguard the Interests of the [Islamic Government] System"*, which gave it strong legitimacy and protection from those powerful elements of the government who had their ideological lingering.

The seriousness and the level of commitment of the government to the family planning program became very clear in early 1989 when Prime Minister Moosavi announced that "*none of the government's development and welfare programs is likely to succeed without a serious family planning program.*" He explicitly referred to the need for a solution to the population problem and referred to figures on Iran's population growth rate as 'alarming' (Moosavi, 1989). In line with this commitment, the Ministry of Health and Medical Education was given the mandate, and almost unlimited resources, to provide free family planning services to all married couples, to promote small family size norms, and to help individual couples keep their family size at a reasonably low level (2 to 3 children). Several other ministries as well as the Islamic Republic of Iran Broadcasting Organization (IRIB) were required to closely cooperate with the Ministry of Health in promoting these objectives. The family planning program officially inaugurated in December 1989, had three major goals: (1) to encourage a spacing of 3 to 4 years between pregnancies; (2) to discourage pregnancy for women aged below 18 and above 35 years; and (3) to limit family size to 3 children. To remove continuing doubts regarding the acceptability of sterilization, in 1990 the High Judicial Council declared that sterilization of men and women was not against Islamic principles or existing laws. This declaration was essential for the promotion of sterilization as a means of population control. The Family Planning Bill, which had been prepared in 1989, was finally ratified by the Parliament in May 1993. The ratification of this Bill not only removed most of the economic incentives for high fertility and large families but it also provided the necessary legal basis for the population control policy. According to the first article of this Law, all social benefits and privileges (including family allowances, social security/health benefits, and maternity leave) allocated according to the number of children will not include the fourth or subsequent child born one year after the passage of the bill. The second article obliged the Ministry of Education to include material dealing with population, maternal and child health in the formal curricula and textbooks of all schools. The third article of the law obliges the IRIB to develop, commission and broadcast radio and TV programs aimed at raising public awareness on maternal and child health and population. According to the fourth article, expenses incurred by different organizations specified in articles 2 and 3 are to be covered by savings made through the application of the first article of the law.

IRANIAN FAMILIES RESPOND TO THE PRAGMATIC POLICY

The family planning program, sponsored by the Islamic Republic State, took great strides towards its main objective of offering eligible couples with a variety of family planning services and contraceptive devices. The responses of the couples can be assessed through a study of contraceptive prevalence rates and an analysis of the basic characteristics of the population covered. The annual Knowledge, Attitude, Practice Surveys carried out by the Ministry of Health and Medical Education during 1989-1997 and the Iran Demographic and Health Survey carried out in 2000 provided a wealth of data on the responses of the families to the policy. The total contraceptive prevalence rates of rural and urban segments of the population shown by various national surveys are summarized in Table 1. By 1992, that is, only three years after the official revival of the family planning program, almost two-thirds of married women aged 15-49 were practicing some form of contraception. Five years later, according to the 1997 KAP survey, the contraceptive prevalence rate had risen to almost 75 per cent. More important, according to the 1977 survey, the contraceptive prevalence rate for urban women (53.8 per cent) was almost two and half times that of rural women (19.9 per cent). In other words, for every rural woman using a contraceptive, there were 2.7 urban women. In contrast, the rural-urban difference in contraceptive prevalence for 1992 is only 23 per cent. This means that, in 1992, for every rural woman using a contraceptive there were only 1.4 urban women. Five years later, according to the 1997 KAP survey, the urban-rural gap had shrunk to only 12 per cent. Even this small advantage was mainly due to the fact that a much larger proportion of the urban couples (23 per cent) as compared with the rural (9 per cent) were using the traditional method of withdrawal. A series of independent surveys carried out by a joint team of Iranian and French researchers in Shiraz county of Fars province in 1996-1998 (Agha et al., 1997; Mehryar et al., 1997; 1999) revealed similarly high contraceptive prevalence rates in both urban and rural areas.

Some traditional methods of contraception, particularly *coitus interruptus* (withdrawal), have been known and practiced in Iran since time immemorial. The use of this method (under the juristic title of *azl*) has been widely discussed (and mostly

Table 1
Contraceptive Prevalence rate among women 15-49 in Iran, 1976-2000

	1976 Method Type			*1989 Method Type*			*1992 Method Type*			*1997 Method Type*			*2000 Method Type*		
	Modern	*Tradi-tional*	*All*	*Modern*	*Tradi-tional*	*All*	*Modern*	*Tradi-tional*	*All*	*Modern*	*Tradi-tional*	*All*	*Modern*	*Tradi-tional*	*All*
Urban	34	21	54	33	31	64	47	27	74	55	23	78	55.2	22.2	77.4
	15	5	20	21	10	31	41	10	51	57	9	66	57.3	9.9	67.2
	24	13	37	30	19	49	45	20	65	55	18	73	56	17.8	73.8

Source: for 1976 see Aghajanian and Gross, 1993; for 1989 through 1997 see Ministry of Health and Medical Education, 1998; for 2000 see Ministry of Health and Medical Education, 2002.

approved) by Muslim jurists. Yet the trend in use of modern contraceptive in a short period of time in both rural and urban areas is a unique experience for a Middle East country.

Contraceptive use behavior, like most other aspects of human behavior, is known to vary according to such major socio-demographic characteristics as age, sex, urban-rural background, and education. Data on some of these variables are available for the 1977 Iran Fertility Survey and the 2000 Demographic and Health Survey (DHS). It would appear that the revived family planning program of Iran has largely reduced the impact of factors such as rural residence and literacy as major barriers to contraceptive use. It is possible that the detailed analysis of DHS data would show very little impact of the conventional socioeconomic variables on contraceptive behavior in Iran in 2000 and beyond.

Family size, measured by total fertility rate has declined significantly along the increasing rate of contraceptive use in Iran during the last decade. Data from various sources compiled in Table 2 showed a sharp decline in total fertility rate in Iran since 1986. For example, the 1991 census data indicated that the total fertility rate of Iranian women had declined from 7.0 to 5.5 during the preceding 5 years. A sharp decline in the number of births registered by the Civil Registration Organization was observed for the same period (Ladier-Fouladi, 1996). The estimated birth fell from 43.4 in 1986 to 30.4 per thousand in 1986. The corresponding decline in total fertility estimates was from 6.2 to 4.2. The results of the 1996 census indicated an even more precipitous decline in family size. The total fertility rate calculated on the basis of the 1996 census was 3.1, which was only 42 per cent of the 1986 total fertility rate. Over the 10 years family size in Iran dropped by over 58 per cent along with the marked increase in contraceptive use observed during the same period. By the year 2000, the total fertility rate for Iran has decreased to an amazing 2 children per woman which is the below replacement fertility level. The rural and urban difference in total fertility rate remained but the gap was remarkably lower than what it was in 1986.

Table 2
Age-specific (per thousand of women aged 15-49) and Total Fertility Rates of Iranian Women, by Place of Residence, 1976-2000

			Total		
Age	*1976*	*1986*	*1991*	*1996*	*2000*
15-19	150	149	108	64	26.8
20-24	316	303	252	191	98.7
25-29	301	313	249	184	122.5
30-34	242	274	211	125	88.5
35-39	169	211	164	73	45.0
40-44	85	112	88	31	14.8
45-49	24	29	28	18	3.2
TFR	6.3	7.0	5.5	3.4	2.0
	Urban				
Age	1976	1986	1991	1996	2000
15-19	123	122	103	58	23.9
20-24	258	232	335	176	89.8
25-29	216	231	212	164	112.8
30-34	145	197	169	114	83.0
35-39	91	143	122	63	37.2
40-44	45	72	62	26	10.4
45-49	13	17	20	18	1.4
TFR	4.4	5.1	4.6	3.1	1.79
	Rural				
Age	1976	1986	1991	1996	2000
15-19	169	157	116	72	32.1
20-24	360	350	300	212	114.7
25-29	359	380	321	226	139.9
30-34	306	340	290	167	97.7
35-39	225	272	237	185	59.2
40-44	111	148	129	45	22.7
45-49	45	40	42	18	6.3
TFR	7.6	8.4	7.1	4.6	7.6

Source: For 1976 to 1996 see Aghajanian and Mehryar, 1999. For 2000 see Ministry of Health and Medical Education, 2002.

CONCLUSION

Revolutions as source of social change influence all domains of individual life. Revolutionaries start their rule, assuming that they will be able to stick to their ideology in resolving various affairs of society, but often only tend to consolidate their power in the establishment of the new state. In Iran the revolutionaries soon noticed that the maintenance and continuity of the new state depended on pragmatism and compromise regarding various issues. The strong return of the Islamic government to development of a family planning policy and implementation of a comprehensive system of contraceptive delivery across urban and scattered rural areas is a perfect example of the vitality of pragmatism for even the most radicalized revolutionary state.

The Iranian experience reviewed here also reflects the continuing impact of the state, regardless of its nature and ideology, in the domain of family. The extensive provision of family planning services and products supplied to the most isolated rural villages in Iran targeted influencing the behavior of couples in limiting the number of children. As much as the welfare of the family and the high quality of children have been emphasized as the official line in the promotion of such services, the ultimate goal of the policy has been to reduce the overall population growth rate; perceived as a threat to economic growth and hence stability of the state and nation.

From the data reviewed here it is obvious that the government has gained results from its effort as reflected in the increasing rate of use of contraceptives, modern and traditional, and the decline of family size and the birth rate. What is interesting and maybe puzzling is the question as to "what were the factors behind such strong familial and individual level motivation for embracing family planning services and reducing family size?" It would be very hard to assume that the family planning program and its limited mass media campaign generated these motivations. Some casual observers have indicated the economic pressure and hardships of ensuing from the Iran-Iraq war as the source of consent and rush for limiting family size. Yet many of the families with relatively large number of children in the past have been families of limited means. What seems to be the most plausible explanation of the motivation behind the desire for smaller family size is the increase in economic aspirations of men and woman and the related materialism associated with such aspirations. This development seems to be competing for the tangible and intangible resources which otherwise would go to the children in ones family.

Another testable hypothesis for future research to consider is the change in the intergenerational wealth flow of the Iranian family. The traditional patriarchal Iranian family has been centered on the older generation and the head of the extended family, and children have had a major role in supporting and protecting the elderly. An emerging trend seems to be families centered on children. Parents are very much interested in the quality of life of their children - at least as measured by their effort toward educating their children. In these child-centered families, parents seem to be directing more of their limited resources for improving the quality of life of their children rather than toward the care of their elders. Hence, there is more incentive to also limit the number of children. Both the economic aspiration hypothesis and the child centered nuclear family hypothesis remain to be tested in the Iranian context.

REFERENCES

Agha, Homa, J-C. Chasteland, Y. Courbage, M. Ladier-Fouladi, and A.H. Mehryar. (1997). Famille et fecondite a Shiraz (1996). Dossiers et Recherches 60. Paris: Institut Nationald' Etudes Demographiques.

Aghajanian, A. (1991). "Population Change in Iran, 1966-86: A Stalled Demographic Transition?" *Population and Development Review,* 17: 703-715.

Aghajanian, A., A.B. Gross, and S.M. Lewis. (1993). Evaluation of Iran Fertility Survey (Working Paper 93-2). University of Washington, Center for Studies in Demography and Ecology.

Aghajanian, A. and A. H. Mehryar. (1999). "Fertility Transition in the Islamic Republic of Iran, 1976-1996." *Asian-Pacific Population Journal,* 14, 1: 21-42. of America, March 29-April 2, New Orleans, La.

Behnam, Dj. (1961). A la Recherche d'une Solution Pour la Pression Demographique: Rapport National d'Iran. Report Presente a la Conference de l'I.P.P.F.

Ladier-Fouladi, M. (1996). "La Transition de la Fecondite en Iran." Population, 51: 1101-1128.

Lapidus, I.M. (1988). A History of Islamic Societies. New York: Cambridge University Press.

Mehryar, A. H. and M. Tabibian. (1997). "Correlates of Fertility Decline in Iran, 1976-1996." Tehran: Institute for Research on Planning & Development. Working Papers Series in English (No 15).

Mehryar, A. H., M. Tabibian, and R. Gholipour. (1999). "Population Policy Change and Fertility Decline in Iran, 1986-1996: A District Level Analysis." Paper presented at the Sixth Scientific Conference, Economic Research Forum, Cairo, Egypt (28-30 October 1999).

Ministry of Health and Medical Education. (1998). A Review of Reproductive Health and Family Planning Indicators in the Islamic Republic of Iran. Tehran: Statistics Unit, Office of the Undersecretary for Public Health, Ministry of Health and Medical Education. (Mimeographed Monograph Persian).

Ministry of Health and Medical Education. (2002). Iran Demographic and Health Survey. Tehran, Iran: Ministry of Health and Medical Education.

Momeni, Dj. (1972). "The Difficulties of Changing the Age at Marriage in Iran". *Journal of Marriage and the Family,* 34(3): 545-551.

Moosavi, M. H. (1989). "Without Population Control We Cannot Do Any of the Other Programs". *Iran Times,* (28 April, 1989).

Nortman, D. and E. Hofstatter. (1979). Population and Family Planning Programs: Supplementary Tables to the Ninth Edition of the Factbook. New York: Population Council (Working Paper, Special Series, and No.2).

——. (1980). Population and Family Planning Programs: A Compendium of Data Through 1978. New York: Population Council.

Plan and Budget Ministry. (1989). The First Plan of Economic, Social and Cultural Development of the Islamic Republic of Iran (1989-1993) Bill, Appendix I. (In Persian). Tehran, Iran: (Plan & Budget Press).

Statistical Center of Iran. (1987). Iran Fertility Survey, 1977. Tehran: Iran Statistical Center. (In Persian).

Statistical Center of Iran. (1988). "National Census of Population and Housing of Iran, 1986." Tehran: Iran Statistical Center (In Persian).

Statistical Center. (1997). "National Census of Population and Housing of Iran, 1996." Tehran: Iran Statistical Center (In Persian).

Statistical Center of Iran. (1998). Demographic indicators of Iran, 1956-1996. Tehran: Iran Statistical Center. (In Persian).

BREASTFEEDING IN THE 21st CENTURY: A THEORETICAL PERSPECTIVE

8

J. Stolzer

THEORETICAL FOUNDATION

Bronfenbrenner's (1999) bioecological theory assumes that all developmental processes are nested within interactive circular systems. Bronfenbrenner has proposed a process-person-context-time model that explains development and those systemic processes that affect the form, power, content, and direction of later developmental trajectories. According to the corollaries contained within Bronfenbrenner's bioecological model, development is shaped by various interactive systems which include the microsystem, the mesosystem, the exosystem, the macrosystem, and the chronosystem. The core theoretical premise of the bioecological model is that development is a function of the forces emanating from all of the various systems and those relationships that exist between the systems.

Bronfenbrenner (1999) has suggested that the concept of historical time is essential to understanding specific developmental pathways as development is embedded and powerfully shaped by specific historical events. Scientific data clearly document that a biocultural shift has occurred with respect to historical breastfeeding patterns, particularly in technologically advanced societies (Dettwyler, 1995; Wolf, 2001). For the vast majority of human existence, mothers have sustained children with human milk. However, the current historical period in which we find ourselves living has witnessed a monumental shift in maternal feeding practices (Dettwyler, 1995).

Bronfenbrenner (1999) has postulated that maternal role expectations are determined by the larger culture. When a culture's expectations of the maternal role change, the predictable result is that maternal behaviors are altered. According to Bronfenbrenner's theory (1989), if the newly acquired maternal behaviors continue over time, developmental outcomes will eventually be altered. This theoretical construct is applicable to breastfeeding as it has been proposed by various scholars that altering ancient breastfeeding patterns may in fact be linked to specific physiological developmental trajectories for mother and child and to an alteration in mother-child attachment processes (Dettwyler, 1995; Jelliffe & Jelliffe, 1978; Malone, Papagni, Ramini, & Keltner, 2004; Palmer, 1991). The lives of family members are interdependent and it is well known that the behaviors of individual family members affect the entire familial system. Bronfenbrenner (1999) has indicated that individual family member's reactions to their societal role in a particular historical time can affect familial development both within and across generational timetables.

Bronfenbrenner (1999) suggests that human development entails dynamic, complex, and reciprocal interaction between an active, evolving biopsychological human organism and the persons, objects, and symbols in its immediate environment. Bronfenbrenner (1995) has conceptualized the immediate environment as the microsystem, and has postulated that the microsystem is the force that propels all developmental processes. Applying this fundamental postulate to the lactation process, parental feeding decisions are hypothesized to originate within the confines of the microsystem. However, breastfeeding in the 21st century cannot be conceptualized as occurring in a vacuum, as a multitude of variables have been found to influence both the initiation and duration of breastfeeding rates across the globe (Stuart-Macadam & Dettwyler, 1995; Wolf, 2001).

Bronfenbrenner's bioecological theory (1999) incorporates the various systems and the interactive nature of these vital systemic processes. Bronfenbrenner's theory is applicable to the study of human lactation in that it defines individual, familial, communal, institutional, contextual, cultural, and historical constructs as imperative to the understanding of developmental processes. According to Bronfenbrenner (1999), the various systems are conceptualized as multidirectional processes; that is the various systems are continually influencing as well as being influenced. For decades, the scientific community has relied on reductionistic, unidirectional linear models as indicators of individual developmental trajectories. Bronfenbrenner has reconceptualized seminal developmental theory as intrinsically intertwined systems that are inherently interactive, multidirectional, and dependent on particular historical events.

Although Bronfenbrenner has explicitly stated that environmental changes across historical time are fundamental to our understanding of development, he also argues that changes occurring in the short term may be equally consequential (1999). Bronfenbrenner points out that changes in developmental trajectories can be seminally linked with family policy, the work environment, the community, and the culture at large (1999). According to Bronfenbrenner (1999), maternal role expectations are determined by extraneous forces; that is maternal scripts are dictated not by the familial sphere alone, but by complex and multifarious forces that are outside of maternal control. Maternal role expectations vary from culture to culture, across historical time, and across contexts (Bronfenbrenner, 1999). In this regard, humans, although constrained by particular historical, cultural, and socioeconomic conditions, are continually influencing developmental outcomes through their own choices and behaviors. Bronfenbrenner's bioecological model takes into account the various nested systems, and recognizes the importance of individual choice when operationalizing developmental processes. Employing Bronfenbrenner's compendious bioecological theory, the following sections will deal with the various systems and how they inherently influence maternal feeding decisions.

THE MICROSYSTEM

The microsystem is defined as "a pattern of activities, roles, and interpersonal relations experienced by the developing person in a given face–to–face setting with particular physical and material features" (Bronfenbrenner, 1989:39). The microsystem includes family, friends, and other interpersonal relationships. The microsystem is characterized by direct, interactional processes as intimate relationships are the cornerstone of this system. Significant others continually influence individual development by altering and/or maintaining particular environments that either encourage optimal developmental processes, or suppress the possibility of optimal developmental trajectories.

The decision to breastfeed or formula feed is most often made within the confines of the microsystem, yet this familial decision is affected by the larger systems. There are many systemic consequences associated with the decision to feed children artificial milk. According to research data, it costs an individual family $1,000-$1,500 a year to formula feed one infant, and this does not include the medical costs associated with artificial feeding (Palmer, 1991). Researchers have found child health and longevity rates are directly affected by the method of feeding that is employed during early childhood. Human milk contains immunological constituents that are absent in both animal milk and laboratory produced formulas, hence the morbidity and mortality rates for artificially fed children are higher than those found in breastfed child populations (American Academy of Pediatrics, (AAP) 2005; Ball & Wright, 1999; Bener, Denic & Galadari, 2001; Malone, et al., 2004; Miller, 2003; Scariati, Grummer– Strawn and Fein, 1997; Sears, Greene, Willan, Taylor, Flannery, Cowan, Herbison, & Poulton, 2002).

The World Health Organization has endorsed breastfeeding as the optimal method of feeding and nurturing children as decades of scientific data confirms that breastfeeding reduces the risks of (1) Diarrhea; (2) Respiratory Infection; (3) Otitis Media; (4) Pneumonia; (5) Urinary Infection; (6) Necrotizing Enterocolitis; (7) Bacterial Infection; (8) Type I and Type II diabetes; (9) Obesity; (10) Celiac Disease; (11) Inflammatory Bowel Disease; (12) Childhood Cancer; (13) Asthma; and (14) Allergies (AAP, 2005; Bener, et al., 2001; Jones & Jones, 2004; Miller, 2003; Sears, et al., 2002; United States Department of Health and Human Services, (HHS) 2000; World Health Organization, 1990).

Breastfeeding enhances immune system functioning, and it has been suggested that longer durations of breastfeeding have been associated with the most positive health outcomes (HHS, 2000; Wolf, 2003). Research has also confirmed that women benefit immensely from breastfeeding. Lactating women have been found to exhibit enhanced hormonal, physical, and psychosocial functioning. Breastfeeding has been found to increase the maternal hormones oxytocin and prolactin, and these hormones have been associated with minimized postpartum blood loss, and rapid uterine involution (AAP, 2005; HHS, 2000). Women who breastfeed experience psychosocial benefits as well as increased maternal self confidence and an increased attachment to ones child has been reported in the medical literature (HHS, 2000; Wolf, 2003). Scientific data also indicate that breastfeeding decreases the likelihood of maternal depression, anxiety, and negative stress response (Mazzacappa, 2004).

Scientific data confirm that breastfeeding suppresses ovulation (AAP, 2005; HHS, 2000; McNeilly, 1993), and breastfeeding for 2 years or longer has been correlated with a reduction in breast and ovarian cancer (HHS, 2000; Wolf, 2003). Breastfed children require fewer doctor's visits and hospitalizations; and prescription drug use is lower in breastfed child populations (HHS, 2000).

Scientific research has confirmed the dangers associated with cigarette smoking. Lung cancer, emphysema, heart attack, and stroke are some of the possible risks associated with tobacco use. However, it is important to note that the Surgeon General of the United States has indicated that breastfeeding is still advisable for women who cannot or will not stop smoking as the benefits associated with human milk outweigh the risks of nicotine exposure (HHS, 2000). Data indicate that formula feeding is a known risk factor for children, and that human milk is far superior, *even* when tainted by the toxins found in cigarettes. The vast majority of the world's inhabitants are aware of the harmful effects associated with cigarette smoking, yet very few understand the risks associated with formula feeding as governments across the world have yet to require a warning label on formula.

A significant number of scholars have postulated that the differences in physiological functioning that are found in breastfed versus artificially fed children are due to the stimulation of the immune system response that is precipitated by the lactation process (Hanson, Korotkova, Lundin, Haversen, Silfverdal, Baltzer, Strandvik, & Telemo, 2003; Lawrence, 1994; Walker, 1993; 2005). What is undeniably clear at this time is that measurable, statistically significant differences exist in artificially fed and breastfed child populations (AAP, 2005; Bener, et al., 2001; HHS, 2000; Jones & Jones, 2004; Lawrence, 1994; Scariati, et al., 1997; Sears, et al., 2002; Wolf, 2003), and these differences can negatively impact microsystemic functioning.

Scholars in the field of human lactation have postulated that microsystemic functioning has been altered by the loss of breastfeeding role models (Stuart-Macadam & Dettwyler, 1995). Throughout the course of human history, the vast majority of females have had numerous family members who they could count on to pass down the "art of breastfeeding". Grandmothers, aunts, sisters, mothers, and cousins were all versed in appropriate breastfeeding management, and these role models were expected to pass their knowledge vertically through the generations. In the past, females were accustomed to seeing family members breastfeed their young and through this sustained exposure, breastfeeding became an intrinsic component of the mothering ethos (Stuart-Macadam & Dettwyler, 1995).

Modern day Westerners have collectively decreed that a woman's worth is based on her economic earning power. In the 21st century, we have become indoctrinated with the "theory of the self"–a theory which emphasizes individual achievement, individual success, and autonomy at any cost. Scholars in the field of human lactation have proposed that this emphasis on the self has contributed to the low rates of breastfeeding in Western cultures (Stuart-Macadam & Dettwyler, 1995). Breastfeeding by its very nature is a mutually dependent relationship as dyadic processes are central to the successful breastfeeding relationship (Dettwyler, 1995). Perhaps it is worth contemplating that a cultural shift in the way we view mothering is called for. The "theory of the self" may best meet the needs of individuals, but when families are involved, perhaps a reexamination of this central component of Western society is needed at this time. Furthermore, a shift in the way we collectively view motherhood may alter systemic processes within the microsystem, which in turn will alter the various proximal systems.

THE MESOSYSTEM

The mesosystem is defined as "the linkages and processes taking place between two or more settings containing the developing person (e.g., the relations between home and school, school and workplace etc.), in other words, a mesosystem is a system of microsystems" (Bronfenbrenner, 1989, p.227).

For over 70 years there has existed scientific evidence that distinct and measurable cognitive differences can be found between breastfed and formula fed children. Studies clearly indicate that children who received human milk out perform their artificially fed cohorts on a number of standardized intelligence tests. Breastfeeding has been correlated with elevated I.Q. scores and increased cognitive performance in both children and adults, and it has been suggested that these statistically significant findings increase with the duration of breastfeeding (AAP, 2005; Anderson, Johnstone & Remax, 1999; Barbas & Kelleher, 2004; HHS, 2000; Hoefer & Hardy, 1929; Mortensen, Michaelsen, Sanders, & Reinisch, 2002; Wolf, 2003).

Research confirms that the length of time spent breastfeeding and I.Q. scores are positively correlated. Strictly controlled studies have found that even when other variables are controlled, (e.g. parental education, socioeconomic status, and infant gestational age), breastfed children score significantly higher on intelligence tests (Fergusson, Beautrais, & Silva, 1982; HHS, 2000; Mortensen, et al., 2002; Rogan & Gladen, 1993). It appears that there exsists a dose–response effect with regard to breastfeeding as those children who were breastfed the longest have been found to exhibit the most significant elevations in I.Q. scores (Mortensen, et al., 2002; Rogan & Gladen, 1993; Wolf, 2003).

Seminal studies have also confirmed that breastfed children are less likely to suffer from learning disorders, language difficulties, and behavioral problems (Broad, 1972; Maslow & Szilagy-Kessler, 1946; Menke, 1977). The enhanced cognitive capacity of breastfed children may be due in part to the constituents of human milk that contain various factors that cannot be duplicated in laboratory settings (AAP, 2005). Docosahexanoic acid (DHA) is essential for optimal brain development, and it may be one of the factors influencing the increase in cognitive abilities and the decrease in behavioral problems found in breastfed child populations (de Andraca & Uauy, 1995; HHS, 2000; Walker, 1993, 2005).

Currently, it is impossible to understand in its totality the composition of human breast milk. Researchers are now just entering the seminal phase of deciphering the biological components that interact during the lactation process. What is clear at the present time is that breastfeeding has been found to be associated with increased child cognitive functioning, fewer behavioral problems in children, and a decrease in learning disorders (Fergusson, et. al., 1982; HHS, 2000; Maslow & Szilagy-Kessler, 1946; Menke, 1977; Rogan & Gladen, 1993; Wolf, 2003). According to Bronfenbrenner's mesosytemic corollary (1989), processes that occur between the various settings can, and often times do lead to familial disruption. A child who is experiencing school difficulties is almost certain to affect the functioning of his or her family. Bronfenbrenner (1989) has postulated that the systems are intrinsically interdependent; when one system is disrupted, a disruption in the larger systems is a certainty. Children who are experiencing cognitive or behavioral problems at school do not exist in isolation as problems at school will reverberate into the various proximal systems.

Another way breastfeeding can be theoretically linked to the mesosystem is by examining the modern-day workforce. One hundred years ago, women were deemed "successful" if they raised happy and healthy children and if their families were content (Golden, 2001). In the 21st century, women are judged by completely different standards. It is no secret that we currently value the worker over the family. If this were not so, we would have a workforce in place that was structured around the familial needs; however, just the opposite is true. We must structure our families around the 9–5 economy, and our children are particularly vulnerable in this type of environment. We have constructed a society that values the worker above the mother, and there exists clear (albeit covert) cultural dictates that women must work outside of the home in order to be perceived as productive citizens (Stuart-Macadam, 1995).

Westerners have also altered mesosystemic functioning by polarizing the public and private spheres. There is a common misperception that the era of the "working woman" has made breastfeeding impractical. The fact of the matter is that women have worked for thousands of years and have breastfed successfully because they were expected to work and mother simultaneously. Relatively recently, the Western world has collectively decreed that the public and private spheres are completely separate–that is work and mothering must never mix. However, breastfeeding is not inherently incompatible with women's work; it is particular cultural belief systems that have artificially mandated that the two could not occur simultaneously (Stuart-Macadam & Dettwyler, 1995).

In spite of the overwhelming scientific evidence that documents the superiority of human milk, it is a possibility that breastfeeding advocates may be accused of being "anti women' and wanting to return women back to the "barefoot and pregnant" place of the past. This assertion can be countered by proposing a cultural worldview shift that honors women for their contributions to the public sphere and *also* for their provision of optimal care for their children (Stuart-Macadam & Dettwyler, 1995). It has been hypothesized that the dichotomy of the public and private spheres has actually prohibited women from excelling in the workplace and this dichotomy has almost certainly diminished woman's biosocial capacity as an irreplaceable force in the life of her child (Van Esterik, 1995). What is clear at the present time is that mesosystemic functioning affects how we raise our children, and in turn, effects the inherent functioning of humanity itself (Bronfenbrenner, 1989).

THE EXOSYSTEM

The exosystem is defined as "the linkages and processes taking place between two or more settings, at least one of which does not ordinarily contain the developing person, but in which events occur that influence processes within the immediate setting that does contain that person" (Bronfenbrenner, 1989, p.227)

A review of the scholarly literature indicates that in Western cultures, physicians are expected to provide parents with the most compendious and accurate information regarding the lactation process. In particular, the Obstetrician, Gynecologist, and the Pediatrician are viewed as the experts in matters surrounding breastfeeding (Golden, 2001; Palmer, 1991; Taveras, Capra, Braveman, Jensvold, Escobar & Lieu, 2003; Wagner, Hulsey, Southgate & Annibale, 2002; Walker, 1993, 2005). However, numerous studies have reported that medical students receive little, if any, education regarding breastfeeding (Freed, 1993, 1995; Stolzer & Hossain, 2005). The physiological process of lactation is often times neglected during the course of medical school training, and problematic conditions (such as insufficient milk production or improper positioning) are rarely, if ever covered in the course of medical school training (Freed, 1993; Stanfield, 1984; Stolzer & Hossain, 2005; Taveras, et al., 2003).

The American Academy of Pediatrics (APA) and the World Health Organization have stated unequivocally that breastfeeding ensures the best possible health, developmental, and psychosocial outcomes for children, yet the prestigious American Academy of Pediatrics continues to align itself with the manufacturers of formula. The APA (1) carries advertisements for formula in its Journal "Pediatrics"; (2) received three million dollars from the formula industry to build its headquarters in the state of Illinois; (3) receives significant contributions from the formula industry that are used to fund major medical conferences and research projects; and (4) receives one million dollars a year in the form of renewable grant monies from the formula industry (Baumslag & Michels, 1995; Riordan & Auerbach, 1993). The Surgeon General of the United States, The American Academy of Pediatrics, The American College of Obstetricians and Gynecologists, the American Academy of Family Physicians, and the World Health Organization have all endorsed breastfeeding as the optimal method of feeding and nurturing children, yet many medical schools around the world are not adequately training physicians in the area of human lactation, and prestigious medical associations continue to profit economically from a product that has been scientifically found to increase morbidity and mortality rate in child populations (Baumslag & Michels, 1995; Freed, 1993; Riordan & Auerbach, 1993; Sears, et al., 2002; Stolzer & Hossain, 2005; Zaghloul, Harrison, Fendley, Pierce, & Morrisey, 2004).

By employing Bronfenbrenner's bioecological systems theory, we can assume that the functioning systems at the various levels are intrinsically interconnected. The processes that occur on one level affect all subsequent levels, thus exosystemic functioning can be linked directly to those processes occurring in the familial environment. Breastfeeding is a complex and circuitous variable, and in order to understand declining breastfeeding rates, each level must be taken into consideration if we are serious in our endeavor to increase breastfeeding rates exponentially.

It is imperative that parents are informed of the various risks associated with formula feeding and that policy makers around the world take into account the myriad of ways in which breastfeeding can affect systemic functioning on all of Bronfenbrenner's proposed levels. Scholars in the field of human lactation have asserted that specific national policies could promote breastfeeding for working mothers. Proposed changes in national policy include a maternal health policy that includes job reinstatement, nursing breaks, and paid leave; flexible work schedules, flextime, part-time, job sharing, an option to work from home; illness related or emergency child care; and various parental leave options (Baumslag & Michels, 1995; Galtry, 2003).

It is undeniable that the various levels proposed by Bronfenbrenner are interdependent. We cannot discuss breastfeeding at the micro level (i.e., familial level) without taking into consideration the impact of proximate levels. In the following section, we shall explore how cultural belief systems have impacted both the initiation and duration of breastfeeding in the Western world.

THE MACROSYSTEM

"The macrosystem consists of the overarching pattern of micro, meso, and exosystems characteristic of a given culture, subculture, or other broader social context, with particular reference to the developmentally instigative belief systems, resources, hazards of life styles, opportunity structures, life course options, and patterns of social interchange that are embedded in each of these systems" (Bronfenbrenner, 1989:228).

Bronfenbrenner (1989) has posited that the macrosystem is a prototype for a particular culture. That is, the macrosystem includes our collective worldview, beliefs, and culturally constructed ideologies. Biologically speaking, it is scientifically clear that mammals have mammary glands in order to feed their offspring with milk produced by their bodies. However, the majority of humans living in industrialized countries have constructed and maintained distinct perceptions of the mammary glands (i.e., the breasts) that are not at all congruent with other mammals, or for that matter, with the majority of other humans living on this planet (Dettwyler, 1995; Palmer, 1991).

Scholars have concluded that breasts are not inherently sexual in the mammalian species and that the West's obsession with the female breast is a culturally induced phenomenon as humans are the only known mammals that include the female breast in copulatory activity (Anderson, 1983). Analyzing Ford and Beach's 1951 study, Dettwyler (1995) has documented that attaching sexual significance to the mammary glands is not a universal practice among humans. Ford and Beach (1951) surveyed 190 cultures from around the globe. Of the 190 cultures sampled, 13 reported that the female breasts were stimulated as part of the sexual act, either as a precursor to sexual intercourse, or as a part of the copulatory act itself. Of these 13 cultures, only 3 reported that female breasts were sexually attractive. The vast majority of cultures sampled reported that the female breast was viewed as life sustaining for children, and that no sexual significance was attached to this specific part of the female anatomy (Ford & Beach, 1951; Dettwyler, 1995).

In Western culture, female breasts are perceived as sexually stimulating for both males and females (Golden, 2001; Palmer, 1991; Van Esterik, 1995; Wolf, 2001). It has been hypothesized that the West's preoccupation with the sexualization of the female mammary glands has led to incongruent feelings about breastfeeding (Hausman, 2003; Palmer, 1991; Wolf, 2001). Of course, if a culture perceives breasts as sexual, it seems reasonable to assume that suckling a child at a sexual part of the anatomy would cause extreme uneasiness. Still, it is worth noting that for the majority of humans on earth, breasts are viewed as life sustainers for children–not as sexually enticing entities. Specific cultural mandates dictate how the breast is perceived, and these societally constructed dictums provide the cultural basis for restricting or encouraging the ancient practice of breastfeeding (Dettwyler, 1995; Ford & Beach, 1951; Hausman, 2003; Wolf, 2001).

Modern day Westerners engage in culturally induced practices which hinder the lactation process. We spend millions of dollars a year to medically alter female breasts so that they will be sexually stimulating. We enlarge, lift, and purchase apparel so as to draw sexual attention to this particular part of the female anatomy. This overt sexualization of the female mammary glands has impacted the way we perceive breastfeeding and has challenged us as a culture to question whether we should even engage in a practice which causes so much cultural and individual dissonance.

Bronfenbrenner (1989) has stated that the macrosystem exerts considerable influence over individual behavior. Each of the various systems is impacted by macrosystemic functioning as the macrosystem is a potent dictator with regard to the more proximal systems. It is clear that macrosystemic functioning is dictating other proximal processes with regard to cultural breastfeeding norms. Women who bottle-feed their children are not expected to feed their children in bathrooms, in specified "bottle feeding areas", or in other locations that are away from other human beings. "Closet Nursing" has become a Western phenomenon in the last 100 years, and this cultural phenomenon can be directly linked to the widespread sexualization of the female breast (Dettwyler, 1995; Palmer, 1991).

It is odd that many cultures readily accept and encourage artificial feeding in spite of the fact that it has been scientifically documented that the use of formula increases the risks of child morbidity and mortality. Researchers in the field have demonstrated that artificial feeding increases the risks of SIDS, cancer, diabetes, hospitalization, obesity, suppressed immune functioning, bacterial infections, viral infections, asthma, allergies, and death, yet Westerners continue to participate in cultural practices which impede the lactation process (AAP, 2005; Bener, et al., 2001; Crespo, Iglesias, Llorca, Granda, Fuentes, Gonzalez, & Rodriguez, 2004; Cunningham, Jelliffe, & Jelliffe, 1991; Fredrickson, Sorenson, Biddle, & Kotelchuck, 1993; HHS, 2000; Jones & Jones, 2004; Miller, 2003; Rogan, 1989; Sears, et al., 2002; Wolf, 2003).

Human beings by their very nature want to be accepted and validated. It is extremely hard to go against the flow of ones culture, even if one has concrete scientific evidence to support ones decision. We cannot alter the fact that we have been heavily influenced by Western ideology and that we have created a culture that has slowly, over time, demanded through the various systemic processes, that we feed our children artificially created milk (Hausman, 2003; Wolf, 2001). We have analyzed how the micro, meso, exo, and macro systems have influenced our collective perception of breastfeeding. Now, let us turn our attention to the Chronosystem.

THE CHRONOSYSTEM

Bioecological theory takes into account the importance of historical time when analyzing human development. Bronfenbrenner has postulated that developmental processes are profoundly altered by the conditions and events that are present in particular historical eras (1999). The breastfeeding literature confirms that an unprecedented biocultural shift has occurred with regard to historical breastfeeding patterns in human populations (Dettwyler, 1995; Golden, 2001; Wolf, 2001). For the vast majority of human existence, mothers have sustained their children with human milk. "Throughout our evolutionary history, the mother – child relationship has been forged and sustained by the breastfeeding link. The millions of years of intimate contact between mothers and children consequent on breastfeeding have resulted in what is basically a physiologic interdependence–each relying on the other for optimum functioning of the various physiological processes" (Stuart-Macadam, 1995:7).

What historical circumstances contributed to the schism in this ancient mother-child bond? To begin to answer this question, we will look to the mechanization of the dairy industry. With the industrial revolution came monumental changes to the various systems. According to Palmer (1991), the industrial revolution made it possible, for the first time in recorded history, to have access to cow milk without owning a cow. The industrial revolution ensured the mass production and distribution of cow milk, but the mass production of this milk was not without its problems. One of the major problems associated with the mechanization of the dairy industry was that huge surpluses of whey were being generated, and no market for the whey had yet been established (Palmer, 1991).

Many people erroneously believe that baby formulas were invented after a complete and thorough review of the composition of human milk was completed. This assumption is false. The fact is that the surplus of whey generated by the dairy industry was the impetus of the modern day formula industry (Palmer, 1991). Scientific data confirm no manufactured formula can duplicate human milk as human milk is produced for a specific child and the constituents change according to the needs of the individual child (AAP, 2005; Lawrence, 1994). Secondly, the milk secreted by a (human) female contains live antibodies, immunologic agents, secretory immunoglobulins, and leukocytes that change from feed to feed depending on the particular physiological needs of her offspring (HHS, 2000; Lawrence, 1994). Formula companies would like us to believe that their product is just as beneficial as human milk, but the fact is that the constituents present in human breast milk can not be duplicated in any laboratory anywhere in the world (HHS, 2000).

All mammals produce "species specific' milk–that is, each species has its own unique composition, yet there exists variation within the species, depending on the needs of the individual nursling (AAP, 2005). Compositionally, differing species of mammals produce milk that is uniquely designed for the optimal growth and development of their particular offspring. Jelliffe and Jelliffe (1978) documented that human milk contains over 100 constituents that are present in different chemical compositions and in different amounts than are found in other species milk.

Historically, the manufacturers of artificial baby milk (i.e., formula) have relied on the method of "trial and error" when creating specific formulas (Jelliffe & Jelliffe, 1978; Walker, 1993, 2005). Nutrients, minerals, vitamins, fat etc... are added or depleted only after detrimental physiological effects are detected in infants and children who had consumed the particular formula (Walker, 1993; 2005). Following is an example of formula alterations:

1. Low carotene levels were detected; led to hypoglycemia.
2. DHA deficiency detected; correlates with lowered I.Q.
3. Chloride deficiency detected; correlated with neural defects.
4. Excess of copper; correlated with cirrhosis.
5. Excessive Iron; found to be correlated with SIDS/ Salmonella.
6. Excessive led; associated with decreased cognitive development.
7. Excessive amounts of protein; Associated with lowered I.Q.
8. Zinc deficiency; correlated with inadequate growth/skin lesions (Walker, 1993; 2005).

Walker (1993, 2005) states, essential ingredients are continually being added to formula and that infants who consumed the formula prior to the addition of the necessary ingredients were ingesting formula that was deficient in substances currently defined as essential for optimal growth and development.

When analyzing milk secreted by various mammals, Jelliffe and Jelliffe (1978) demonstrated that horse milk is compositionally closer to human milk than is cow milk; however, it is important to note that horse milk and human milk vary dramatically (See Table 1). If formula companies are sincere in their effort to replicate human milk as closely as possible, shouldn't they be using horse milk instead of cow milk as the base for their formula? Palmer (1991) answers this question by stating that economics is what is at the heart of any industry seeking to profit from the sale of their product, and horse milk based formula would not sell as it is considered culturally unacceptable to drink horse milk in Western culture. Conversely, formula's based on cow milk tend to sell extremely well-particularly in Western culture in spite of the fact that dairy products are the most common allergen in infant populations (Dettwyler, 1995). It is a scientifically accepted fact that cow milk (and soybeans for that matter), when compared to human milk, contain differing biological and biochemical constituents. Formula, regardless of the ingredients added to the bovine or soy base in a laboratory setting, cannot duplicate the milk that is produced by the (human) female (HHS, 2000; Jelliffe & Jelliffe, 1978; Walker, 1993; 2005).

Table 1

Species	*Days Required to Double Birth Weight*	*Fat*	*Protein*	*Lactose*	*Ash*
Human	180	3.8	0.9	7.0	0.2
Horse	60	1.9	2.5	6.2	0.5
Cow	47	3.7	3.4	4.8	0.7
Reindeer	30	16.9	11.5	2.8	0.0
Goat	19	4.5	2.9	4.1	0.8
Sheep	10	7.4	5.5	4.8	1.0

Hambraeus, 1977:17

It appears that the technological advances associated with the industrial revolution changed our collective Western worldview. Anything associated with pre-industrial society was considered "old fashioned", and the new technological advances were heralded as the beginning of a new and brighter era (Palmer, 1991; Wolf, 2001). In tandem with our insatiable thirst for technology came the explosion of advertising for "high tech" baby milk in the 1930s. During the 1940s- 1950s, worldwide breastfeeding rates plummeted as women all over the industrialized world began to feed their children with laboratory-produced formula. Breastfeeding rates dropped from 95% with weaning occurring at 2-3 years of age in the early 1900s to less than 25% in the 1960s (Stuart-Macadam & Dettwyler, 1995).

The cultural custom of feeding (human) children with artificially produced milk has two prerequisites; milk other than human milk must be readily available, and the use of nonhuman milk must be culturally acceptable (Riordan & Auerbach, 1993). Feeding developing offspring with another mammal's milk is a relatively new phenomenon as mammals have been sustaining their young with milk secreted from their bodies since the beginning of the Mesozoic Era, approximately 100 million years ago (Riordan & Auerbach, 1993).

We have changed much in the last 100 years in terms of culturally constructed breastfeeding ideologies. Formula feeding our children is undeniably culturally acceptable, while breastfeeding is culturally questionable–particularly if breastfeeding occurs outside of culturally constructed perimeters. Bronfenbrenner suggests that culturally constructed norms change over time, and these changes can lead to considerable alterations within and across the various systems, thus profoundly affecting individual developmental trajectories (1999).

CONCLUSION

Bronfenbrenner has suggested that developmental processes are nested within interactive, circular systems and the relationships that result from the joint functioning of these various systems (i.e., the Micro, Meso, Exo, Macro, and Chronosystems). Later development is assumed to be a function of early, proximal processes. Traditional theories would lead one to believe that environment alone is responsible for individual trajectories. Bronfenbrenner refutes reductionistic environmentalism and proposes instead an integral, multifarious theory which takes into account all of the various systems, and defines those systems as inherently interactive and powerful.

Breastfeeding is a bioecological phenomenon. We cannot hope to increase our understanding of the complexities surrounding the topic of breastfeeding without taking into account all of the various systems and the interactive nature of these systems. Perhaps by increasing our collective understanding of the various systemic processes that in fact precipitate our cultural ideologies surrounding the topic of breastfeeding; we can increase breastfeeding rates exponentially, and in doing so, affect change on a vast scale.

REFERENCES

American Academy of Pediatrics (AAP), (2005). Policy Statement: Breastfeeding and the Use of Human Milk. *Pediatrics,* 115 (2).

Anderson, E.W., Johnstone, B., & Remax, D. (1999). Breastfeeding and Cognitive Development: A Meta-Analysis. *American Journal of Clinical Nutrition,* 70: 525-535.

Anderson, P. (1983). The Reproductive Role of the Human Breast. *Current Anthropology,* 24 (1): 25-45.

Ball, T.M.and Wright, A.L. (1999). Health Care Costs of Formula Feeding in the First Year of Life. *Pediatrics,* 103(4), 870-876.

Barbas, K., and Kelleher, D. (2004). Breastfeeding Success among Infants with Congenital Heart Disease. *Pediatric Nursing,* 30 (4): 111-117.

Baumslag, N., & Michels, D.L. (1995). Milk, Money, and Madness. The Culture and Politics of Breastfeeding. London: Bergin and Garvey.

Bener, A., Denic, S., and Galadari, S. (2001). Longer Breastfeeding and Protection against Childhood Leukemia and Lymphomas. *European Journal of Cancer,* 37, 234-238.

Broad, F. (1972). The Effects of Infant Feeding on Speech Quality. *New Zealand Medical Journal,* 82:373-375.

Bronfenbrenner, U. (1989). Ecological Systems Theory. *Annals of Child Development,* 6, 187-249.

Bronfenbrenner, U. (1999). Environments in Developmental Perspective: Theoretical and Operational Models. In S. Friedman and T. Wachs (Eds.), Measuring Environment Across the Lifespan (pp. 3-28). Washington, D.C.: American Psychological Association.

Bronfenbrenner, U. (1995). Developmental Ecology through Space and Time: A Future Perspective. In P. Moer, G. Elder, Jr., and K. Lusher (Eds.), Examining Lives in Context: Perspectives on the Ecology of Human Development (p. 619-647). Washington, D.C.: American Psychological Association.

Crespo, R., Iglesias, R., Llorca, J., Granda, L., Fuentes, M., Gonzalez, M., and Rodriguez, M. (2004). Breastfeeding and the Risk of Hospitalization for all Causes and Fever of Unknown Origin. *European Journal of Public Health,* 14 (3):230-237.

Cunningham, A., Jelliffe, D., and Jelliffe, E.F.P. (1991). Breastfeeding and Health in the 1980s; A Global Epidemiologic Review. *Journal of Pediatrics,* 118(5), 659-676.

de Andraca, I., and Uauy, R. (1995). Breastfeeding for Optimal Mental Development. *World Review of Nutrition and Dietetics,* 78:1-27.

Dettwyler, K. (1995). Beauty and the Breast: The Cultural Context of Breastfeeding in the United States. In P. Stuart-Macadam & K. Dettwyler (Eds.), Breastfeeding: Biocultural Perspectives. New York: Aldine DeGruyter.

Fergusson, D.M., Beautrais, A., & Silva, P.A. (1982). Breastfeeding and Cognitive Development in the First Seven Years of Life. *Social Science & Medicine,* 16:1705-1708.

Fredrickson, D.D., Sorenson, J.R., Biddle, A.K., & Kotelchuck, M. (1993). Relationship between Sudden Infant Death Syndrome and Breastfeeding Intensity and Duration. *American Journal of Diseases in Childhood,* 147 (May):460-462.

Freed, G.L., Clark, S.J., Sorenson, J., Cefalo, R., & Curtis, P. (1995). National Assessment of Physician's Breastfeeding Knowledge, Attitudes, Training, and Experience. *Journal of the American Medical Association,* 273 (6): 472-476.

Freed, G. (1993). Time to Teach What We Preach. *Journal of the American Medical Association,* 269 (2); 243-245.

Ford, C.S., & Beach, F.A. (1951). Patterns of Sexual Behavior. New York: Harper and Row.

Galtry, J. (2003). The Impact on Breastfeeding of Labour Market Policy and Practice in Ireland, Sweden, and the USA. *Social Science and Medicine,* 57:167-177.

Golden, J. (2001). A Social History of Wet Nursing in America. Ohio State University Press.

Hambraeus, L. (1977). Proprietary Milk versus Human Breast Milk: A Critical Approach from the Nutritional Point of View. *Pediatric Clinics of North America,* 24:17-20.

Hanson, L., Korotkova, M., Lundin, S., Haversen, L., Silfverdal, S., Baltzer, I., Strandvik, B., and Telemo, E., (2003). The Transfer of Immunity from Mother to Child. New York Academy of Sciences, 987:199-206.

Hausman, B. (2003). Mother's Milk: Breastfeeding Controversies in American Culture. Routledge, New York.

Hoefer, C., & Hardy, M. (1929). Later Development of Breastfed and Artificially Fed Infants. *Journal of the American Medical Association,* 9:615-618.

Jelliffe, D., & Jelliffe, E.F.P. (1979). Human Milk in the Modern World. Oxford, England: Oxford University Press.

Jones, B., & Jones, S. (2004). Breastfeeding and the Prevalence of Asthma and Wheeze in Children; Analyses from the Third National Health and Nutrition Examination Survey-Prediction and Prevention. *Pediatrics,* 114 (1):S520-S522.

Lawrence, R. (1994). Breastfeeding: A Guide for the Medical Profession (4th Ed.). St. Louis, MO: C.V. Mosby.

Lucas, A., Morley, R., Cole, T., Lister, G., & Leeson-Payne, C. (1992). Breast Milk and Subsequent Intelligence Quotient in Children Born Pre-Term. Lancet, 339:261-264.

Malone, K., Papagni, K., Ramini, S., & Keltner, N. (2004). Antidepressants, Antipsychotics, Benzodiazepines, and the Breastfeeding Dyad. *Perspectives in Psychiatric Care,* 40:73-80.

Maslow, A., & Szilagy-Kessler, I. (1946). Security and Breastfeeding. *Journal of Abnormal and Social Psychology,* 41:83-85.

McNeilly, AS. (1993). Lactational Amenorrhea. Endocrinological Metabolism Clinics of North America, 22 (1):59-73.

Menke, J.H. (1977). Early Feeding History of Children with Learning Disorders. Developmental Medicine and Child Neurology, 19:169-170.

Mezzacappa, E. (2004). Breastfeeding and Maternal Stress Response and Health. *Nutrition Reviews,* 62 (7):261-296.

Miller, K. (2003). Breastfeeding and Risk for Respiratory Disease in Infants. *American Academy of Family Physicians,* 68: 1412-1416.

Mortensen, E., Michaelsen, K., Sanders, S., & Reinisch, J. (2002). The Association between Duration of Breastfeeding and Adult Intelligence. *Journal of the American Academy of Child and Adolescent Psychiatry,* 41:1305-1311.

Palmer, G. (1991). The Politics of Breastfeeding. London: Harper Collins.

Riordan, J., & Auerbach, K. (1993). Breastfeeding and Human Lactation. London: Jones and Bartlett.

Rogan, W.J., & Gladen, B.C. (1993). Breastfeeding and Cognitive Development. *Early Human Development,* 31:181-193.

Rogan, W.J. (1989). Cancer from PCB's in Breast Milk? A Risk-Benefit Analysis. *Pediatric Research,* 25: 105-110.

Scariati, P.D., Grummer-Strawn, L.M., & Fine, S.B. (1997). A Longitudinal Analysis of Infant Morbidity and the Extent of Breastfeeding in the United States. *Pediatrics,* 99 (6), 5.

Sears, M., Greene, J., Willan, A., Taylor, D., Flannery, E., Cowan, J., Herbison, G., & Poulton, R. (2002). Long Term Relation between Breastfeeding and Development of Atopy and Asthma in Children and Young Adults; A Longitudinal Study. *The Lancet,* 360: 901-903.

Stanfield, J.P. (1994). Training of Doctors in Maternal and Child Health (MCH) in Medical School. *Advances in International Maternal and Child Health,* 4: 96-109.

Stolzer, J., & Hossain, S. (2005). Physician Breastfeeding Education: A Regional Assessment. *The Female Patient,* 30: 24-30.

Stuart-Macadam, P., & Dettwyler, K. (1995). Breastfeeding: Biocultural Perspective. New York: Aldine DeGruyter.

Stuart-Macadam, P. (1995). Biocultural Perspectives on Breastfeeding. In P. Stuart-Macadam & K. Dettwyler (Eds.), Breastfeeding: Biocultural Perspective. New York: Aldine DeGruyter.

Taveras, E., Capra, A., Braveman, P., Jensvold, N., Escobar, G., & Lieu, T. (2003). Clinician Support and Psychosocial Risk Factors Associated with Breastfeeding Discontinuation. *Pediatrics,* 112, 108-112.

U.S. Department of Health and Human Services (HHS, 2000). Blueprint for Action on Breastfeeding. Washington, D.C.

Van Esterik, P. (1995). The Politics of Breastfeeding: An Advocacy Prospective. In P. Stuart-Macadam & K. Dettwyler (Eds.), Breastfeeding: Biocultural Perspective. New York: Aldine DeGruyter.

Wagner, C., Hulsey, T., Southgate, M., & Annibale, D. (2002). Breastfeeding Rates at an Urban Medical University after Initiation of an Education Program. *Southern Medical Journal,* 95, 909-910.

Walker, M. (1993). A Fresh Look at the Risks of Artificial Infant Feeding. *Journal of Human Lactation,* 9 (2), 97-107.

Walker, M. (2005). Summary of Hazards of Infant Formula, III. International Lactation Consultant Association.

Wolf, J. (2001). Don't Kill Your Baby. Public Health and the Decline of Breastfeeding in the 19th and 20th Centuries. Ohio State University Press.

Wolf, J. (2003). Low Breastfeeding rates and Public Health in the United States. *American Journal of Public Health,* 93, (12).

World Health Organization (1990). Innocenti Declaration on the Protection, Promotion, and Support of Breastfeeding. Florence, Italy.

Zaghloul, S., Harrison, G., Fendley, H., Pierce, R., & Morrisey, C. (2004). Correlates of Breastfeeding Initiation in Southeast Arkansas. *Southern Medical Journal,* 97, 446-450.

BANGLADESHI MUSLIMS IN MONTREAL: A CASE OF DIVIDED LOYALTY

9

Roksana Nazneen

INTRODUCTION

The Muslims have been in North America for centuries, but Bangladeshis started to immigrate to Canada only in 1960s. These new immigrants were mostly professionals with university education. Their Canadian-born children are now young adults with a very different sense of ethnic identity than their parents.

This study is a follow-up from the initial research that was carried out in 2000. The objective of my initial study was to identify the values that are most likely to be abandoned, undergo adaptation or remain constant (in case of Bangladeshi immigrants in Montreal), and to explain the influence of the intervening variables, such as, length of residence in Canada, regionalism, levels of education and the last years of schooling and occupation on them.

The identity question is central to the Muslim presence in Canada. Bangladeshis, as opposed to East Indians, perceive their own culture in static terms and they view change in it as a possible or inevitable source of danger to the retention of their distinctive value system. These immigrants are trying to follow and adapt to the religious revolution that has been taking place in Bangladesh for the last few years. With the oil-rich Islamic states as potential foreign-aid donors, Bangladesh with a predominantly Muslim population has been making use of the Islamic fraternity in recent years and Bangladeshi ex-patriots have been observing this trend. In 1977, five years after the liberation of the country, Islam was introduced into the Bangladeshi Constitution, and in 1988 an amendment to the

Constitution affirmed Islam the state religion of Bangladesh. General Ziaur Rahman replaced the outwardly secular "Bengali Nationalism" propounded by its founding father, Sheikh Mujibur Rahman, with "Bangladeshi nationalism"–the term highlights the Muslim identity of the country, differentiating its Muslim majority Bengalis from the Hindu Bengalis in India. It seems, after the failure of the Mujib government, his military successors, Zia (1975-1981) and Ershad (1982-1990), realized the importance of "political Islam" to legitimize their rule (Hashmi, 2005).

In my initial study, I was intrigued to find out that the cultural value system of Bangladeshi immigrants living in Montreal was very intimately linked with their religious value system. This trend is especially stronger among women; religion was the most important factor in their lifestyles. Knowing that Bangladeshi families are not living in an insular world, they are apt to look for an alternative culture to combat a utilitarian ideology among the new generation of Bangladeshis. Perhaps for this reason they are increasingly turning towards religion and thus, are becoming more religious in their adopted country than they were in Bangladesh (Rahim, 1990). In recent years, the children of Bangladeshi immigrants in Canada, just like their counterparts in the U.S., have grown up in an increasingly anti-Muslim environment. An American Muslim Council (AMC) poll found that the most disliked religious group in the U.S. was Muslims (Cooper, 1993). The media often has been openly hostile against Muslims while covering the Gulf War, the September 11 attacks (Karim, 2000) or the current war in Iraq. Research carried out in the seventies or eighties also support the position that radio, film, television, school curricula, and church materials also carry profound anti-Muslim messages (Abu-Laban, 1975; Kenny, 1975; Said, 1981). Akram (2005) and Helly (2004) have carefully recorded the post-9/11 incidents of discrimination against various Arab/Muslim communities in the U.S. and in Canada.

The *Instrumentalist* perspective of ethnicity defines ethnicity as a means to an end; and ethnicity persists because it provides a way to cope with specific social conditions, including the globalizing demands of contemporary society. This perspective points to ethnicity as a tool for individuals to avoid the pressures of increased competitiveness, competing value systems or perceived decadence. According to this perspective, a commitment to ethnicity allows an escape from feelings or irrelevance and powerlessness. Appeals to ethnicity foster a sense of relief, continuity, belonging, importance, and security, for those without alternative channels for coping with societal stress (Fleras and Elliot, 2002).

My objective is to present my findings based on two main questions:

1. Why are some of the Canadian-born children of the immigrant parents embracing Islam in order to develop their self-identity?
2. Can instrumental thesis of ethnic identity efficiently explain this phenomenon?

METHOD

As a community member, I have been well aware of the history of the Bangladeshi population in Montreal. For this study I sought information about the adaptive processes pursued by individuals within the community. For example, what does being a Bangladeshi-Muslim in Montreal involve? How do they define Islamic/Bangladeshi identity in North America and if there were any changes since 9/11? How do individuals living within their family and community network adapt to the complex host society of Montreal? I was interested in the extent to which being Bangladeshi is important for one's sense of identity. I also intended to see how their identity may be modified in the process of adaptation, especially since 9/11. The analysis is focused on family units and individual family members.

Data Collection

Data for this study were gathered through participant observation and interviews.

Participant Observation: I have been observing members of the Bangladeshi community and socially interacting with various members of this group since 1988, and have been collecting data since 1995, when I decided to work on this particular topic. My participation in the community has been crucial to my research in several respects. First, I have gained a sense of the activities associated with different social/religious events, who attends them, and the various concerns and preoccupations of community members. Secondly, and in conjunction with reading of secondary literature, my reflections on this information have assisted in clarifying the research problem, in formulating questions, in determining selection criteria, and in guiding interviews. Third, I believe I have become recognized as a trustworthy person to my subjects who, they believed, was not only a member of the community, but as someone who takes an interest in the community. Finally, continuing to socialize with my respondents permitted me to keep in touch with them and follow-up with any research related matters-as I indeed did.

Interviewing within the Community: The interviews I carried out for this research were of three types; pre-test and background interviews followed by in-depth interviews, and lastly, follow-up interviews. I selected 10 families of different age groups, occupation, education level and arrival date in Canada. I used fictitious names in order to protect their identities. The first interview took place in May 1999 while subsequent ones were held between July 1999 and December 1999. The follow-up interviews were held between January and February 2000. After the 9/11 disasters, I went back for the second set of follow-up interviews between July 2002- May 2003. This time I only interviewed members of three families (Ahmed, Hamid and Enam). I was interested in seven (two males and five females) of the Canadian-born unmarried adult children in these families who live with their parents, and consider themselves 'Muslims,' rather than being `Bangladeshi-Canadians'.

Overview of the Respondents

AHMED FAMILY:
Ali: 28-year old male, works full time
Amina: 26-year old female, full time university student, works part-time
Afsana: 22-year old female, full time university student, works part-time

HAMID FAMILY:
Hasib: 27-year old male, university graduate, part-time university student
Hasna: 25-year old female, university graduate, unemployed

ENAM FAMILY:
Eliza: 24-year old female, recent university graduate
Elma: 18-year old female, CEGEP[1] student.

As a Bangladeshi myself, I was aware of the fact that, culturally, Bangladeshis can be very guarded about their privacy. Having maintained constant contact with my respondents, I had developed a close and trusting relationship with these families. Yet, I have also been sensitive to how my proximity to these families might affect my interpretations and assessment. While the concentration on such a small number of respondents does not permit generalization of Bangladeshi immigrants in other social contexts, I do hope to provide a detailed analysis of how some of the Canadian-born adult children of Bangladeshi origin perceive their identity differently than others especially in the wake of 9/11 attacks.

ETHNIC IDENTITY FACTORS

One of the most basic elements in the history and development of a social group is the maintenance of its identity. In multicultural Canada, where group identification can be defined politically, linguistically, culturally, ethically or racially, the political and cultural pluralism promoted does not necessarily put an end to the feelings and perceptions of religious identity and affiliation. Both religion and family tend to be central to personal identity and sense of social support (Hargrove, 1983). Not surprisingly, religion can provide an ideological framework and a codified assurance of kinship reliability and empowerment (Abu-Laban, 1991).

Ethnic identity can be defined as a positive personal attitude and attachment to a group with whom the individual believes he/she has a common ancestry based on shared cultural traits and shared socio-political experiences. According to Rahim (1990: 8):

> ...Bangladeshis had a strong sense of belonging to the culture of Bangladesh. Their mannerisms, customs, and method of social interaction were distinctly Bangladeshi and made little sense to an outsider. They had all retained some essential identity of their native land.... It appeared that the demands of Canadian way of life were imposed on them, and contradictions were apparent in every aspect of their lives. They looked forward and backward but without living in the past. Rather, I believe, they found pleasure and security in their traditions, which were remarkably self-contained.

Muslims from diverse backgrounds in Canada have been nourishing a bicultural identity just like many other immigrant groups. But in the case of the Muslims, the identity they share became stereotyped in recent years, and they now find themselves in a situation where they are constantly asking themselves: "Are we Canadian?" "Are we Muslims?" "Can we be both?"

> It is hard. It is very, very hard to live everyday of your life trying to "prove" that you are Canadian.... Some of us first generation Canadians just don't "fit the part" in their (not all, mind you but some) eyes, they can't fathom how we, odd looking creatures with odd shades of skin in sometimes odd pieces of clothing, eating odd concoctions of food–can be Canadian" (I still haven't figured out what the "average" Canadian is (Khan, 2005).

Some sociologists (e.g., Simon, 1975; Driedger 1977) have identified differences in language and religion as the most important factors that generate conflict and tensions in a multicultural society. These two factors are also the same key variables that reinforce the sense of one's ethnic identity as well. Simon's argument appears to be more significant when we realize that conflict occurs only in the 'wake of progress'. For example, ethnic conflict can surface when there is pressure on minorities to assimilate or attempts to exert what is perceived as illegitimate control. The current socio-political scene, culminating since the Gulf War and augmented by the 9/11 disasters, has served as a breeding ground for ethno-religious conflict. First generation Muslim Canadians are constantly struggling with the issue of a divided-loyalty, and many Canadian Muslims are re-inventing their Islamic identity while their Canadian identity has been challenged or being questioned by the mainstream society.

In case of newly arrived immigrants, the observance of religion can either ease the process of adaptation or strengthen resistance to assimilation. In case of some of the first generation Canadian-born children of Bangladeshi immigrants, the latter seems to be the case.

STRENGTHENING RELIGIOUS VALUES

The maintenance of Bangladeshi-Islamic identity is an important concern for all ten families. The parents are equally concerned about raising their children in a 'free-sex'[2] society where the moral codes are completely different than their own. The parents are generally worried about 'western' cultural practices, especially dating and alcohol consumption. Parents make sure that the children learn the basic Islamic values early on their lives; all the children from these ten families, at some point of their lives, were sent to Sunday schools for religious teachings.

It is not uncommon for parents to resist assimilation of their children by regulating the interaction between their children and other non-Muslim Canadian children. Instead, they encourage their children to forge friendship with other Muslims. The parents from eight of the ten families were worried that Canadian values are contradictory to Bangladeshi-Islamic values, and believed it was better not to expose their children to these values. Their concern mainly revolves around the issues of dating, sex-education at school, consuming alcohol, nudity and violence in the media. These parents appeared very insular as only one of the parents socialized outside the Bangladeshi community, and this association too was limited as it involved Muslims from Pakistani. This trend reflects on the children's social interaction pattern as well. Except for two children from one family, the children tended socialize almost exclusively with friends from their own Bangladeshi community with some limited association with Muslims from India, Pakistan, or Arabs. Nine of the ten families live in predominantly Muslim-areas amid other Bangladeshi immigrants. Elma tries to explain the in-group interaction pattern from her own perspective:

> I never felt comfortable socializing with white[3] class mates. Because of my *religious convictions, I can't go out with them to the clubs, I can't drink or eat pork with them. I can't date. We don't have much in common.*

All the children observed the religious taboo against the consumption of pork. Initially I had three families (Ahmed, Saber and Kamal), where the families only ate *halal* food and strictly observed other religious rituals. Interestingly enough, since September 2000 children from two other families (Hamid and Enam) became strict *halal*-eaters. Hasib, the 27-year old son of Mr. and Mrs. Hamid, used to go to the mosque for weekly Friday prayer. Soon after the 9/11 incidents, he begin going to the mosque five times a day. He started to wear Islamic clothing more often and has grown a beard. He considers himself a 'Muslim', rather than a 'Canadian' or 'Bangladeshi-Canadian' as is the case for five out of other six respondents. Cyber Islam became a great support system for North American Muslims, with Frequently Asked Questions posted on websites like *www.theprophetonline.com* or *www.islam.org* where Muslims from all over the globe communicate. The Canadian-born youth from these three families are familiar with these websites and members of more than one North American Islamic organizations. The universities they attend, have attended or the CEGEPs they go to or have attended, have Islamic associations with designated prayer rooms. All of the young adults from these three families are active members of these associations, even though some of them have graduated from these institutions. Hasib sounds frustrated when he says:

> We have to re-invent our identity as Muslims in North America. We live in a non-Islamic country, yet we are not allowed to date or socialize with the opposite sex. How are we supposed to find our partners? I don't want my parents to find a bride for me when I am in my late twenties!... We meet other Muslims at the association, this is an outlet for us where we communicate about our problems. We have to renegotiate our Islamic identity in North America. Islamic Associations should promote separate Islamic educational institutions for Muslims where they would be able to socialize with other Muslims and eventually would find life-partners. This is very important for the survival of the group.... This will stop intermarriages.

Elma thinks that it is very important to have Islamic network for young Muslims in North America:

> It is high time that we unite together and let these ignorant (non-Muslims) people know that we are not terrorists. We are peace loving people. There is no place for terrorism in Islam. It is our duty to promote the true nature of Islam in North America, so people would get rid of the stereotypes. It is absolutely necessary for us to come together as a group.

All of the seven youth believe that their Muslim identity is more important than their 'Bangladeshi' identity. Mrs. Enam has a mixed reaction:

> I am very proud of my children. This is exactly what we have been trying to do all these years–to make them good Muslims. But I want them to concentrate on their education and career... there is no need to focus too much on religion at this age. When you retire and get old, you do all those things...not when you are young!

Since 9/11 there has been a growing tension between the parents and the children from these particular families. The parents are not very keen about their children's choice of wearing religious gear in public even though they had been encouraging their children to adhere Islamic practices all through their lives. Mrs. Ahmed explains:

> Wearing *hijab* would make them vulnerable to discrimination....They have Mulsim names, isn't that enough? I do not allow my son to grow a beard. The situation has changed since 9/11. We became "terrorist" overnight. ... It is our duty to protect our children.

In my initial study, Mrs. Ahmed spoke strongly about the importance of practicing Islam for her children. But since 9/11, she has changed her position on this issue. Ali, the 28-year old son of Mr. And Mrs. Ahmed, is not allowed to stay at the mosque after the *jamat.*[4] Mrs. Ahmed is not happy with the mosque administrators:

> I told them that the mosque is there for us to go there and pray. They have no business brainwashing my son. Mosques should stay away from the politics.... I send my son there to pray, not to learn about social injustice. We are here (Canada) to stay, instead of fighting the society we should learn how to get along. If we become more militant it will bring only misery to the Muslim community.

But the son does not feel the same way:

> I don't understand... my parents are sending me mixed messages. They taught me to go to the mosque to pray and now they are discouraging me from going there? Why? I meet other Muslims there and we talk about our problems. What is so wrong about that? We have to be united in order to protect our religion. Our parents don't understand how hard it is to be a Muslim these days! It is not about competing in the job market, rather, it is about fighting for our existence.

Mrs. Ahmed further assert:

> My son is not self-sufficient yet, but these people at the mosque are encouraging him to get married. They even found a bride for him!

Ali's reaction:

> We are not allowed to date or to socialize with Muslim girls. Then what is wrong in marrying a decent Muslim girl? My parents should be happy that I don't want to marry a Canadian (non-Muslim)!

The religious values and practices as well as values concerning drinking alcohol, dating and courtship remained almost intact for the first generation Bangladeshi immigrants over time. The religious values remain the same in the second generation of Canadian-born children as well, in some cases it grew even stronger. The values concerning social interactions with other

'Canadians' remain very much alike in both generations, both parents and children socialize within the community or with other Muslim communities.

LOSING BANGLADESHI IDENTITY

At the same time, while religious values seem to remain strong or growing stronger among second generation Bangladeshis, other cultural values are changing. Use of Bengali language has become symbolic for the Canadian-born children. Occasionally they use Bengali[5] with their parents and with other community members[6], but their first language is either English or French. All of the Canadian-born children use English or French to communicate with each other and with their friends. Further, although they all learned how to read and write Arabic in Sunday Schools[7], none of them know how to read or write Bengali. With the exception of one family that migrated to Canada about two years ago, the children from all of the families expressed a dislike for speaking Bengali. It is worth noting that the parents have also been more focused on religious teachings rather than promoting Bengali lessons for their children.

All the parents in this study are first-generation immigrants, and it was the women who showed more evidence of being the custodians of religious and cultural practices. While the parents tend to be settled in their Bengali cultural traditions and customs, the children are more inclined to incorporate non-Bengali tastes into their everyday life experiences. (For example, the children typically prefer 'Canadian' [but *halal*] food over Bengali, and– except for Bengali social gatherings-will typically gravitate to dressing in sober western styles.) The children's entertainment tastes have little, if any, Bengali preferences. During their childhood, these Canadian-born children all had short stints visiting Bangladesh, and many of them do not have clear recollections of their visit. Even though their parents often make trips to Bangladesh, grown-up children are not likely to accompany them. Canadian-born children also do not have a very positive image of Bangladesh. Eliza, the 25-year old daughter from Enam family explains:

> Bangladesh is poor... right? Lots of floods... mosquitoes! I get sick when I go there. Last time my mother had to come back here on an emergency basis in order to get me proper treatment. I don't go to Bangladesh anymore.

Just like most of the Canadian-born children, the 18-year old son of Mr. And Mrs. Uddin, a high-school dropout, does not identify himself as a Muslim-Bangladeshi-Canadian:

> I am Canadian. Yes. I am Canadian. What is the big deal about it?
> ...My parents are Bengali, I am nothing like my parents.

In the home, these children (and parents) gravitate toward Indian Bollywood/Hindi entertainment, which is also readily accessible through cable and satellite. In essence, they have lost physical and emotional contact with Bangladesh; they lack a clear sense of Bangladeshi identity even though their Muslim identity has remained strong. The children from the Ahmed, Enam and Hamid families consider themselves Muslims first, and Canadian second, and they find these identities in contradiction. They are frustrated with U.S. and Canadian foreign policy toward Muslim countries. A large cross-section of Muslims find themselves victimized, misunderstood and powerless in North America. Indeed, though the North American Muslims population has grown significantly in recent years, Muslims typically find their concerns not reflected in policies toward the Muslim world (see Mazrui 1996). Mazrui (1996) further notes that even though North American Muslims are politically active, they respond to policy making from four different identities: their national identity, their racial identity, their religious identity as Muslims, and as American immigrants (or as indigenous Americans). This might further suggest that American Muslims are still trying to reconcile their various identities.

LOOKING FOR A SOURCE OF POWER

Bangladeshi-Canadians belongs to a minority group. Bangladeshis have not been accepted by mainstream society as equal partners and they are somewhat alienated from the society where they live and work (Rahman, 1990). As a group, North American Muslims are afraid of the possibility of being assimilated into American/Canadian society. They want recognition of their religious rights by the society and by the government. As Hasina puts it:

> This is supposed to be multicultural society. But how come we can't celebrate our religious holidays? Even in the States there

> are mainstream educational institutions that observe Islamic holidays.[8] Then why can't we?

All of the Canadian-born children from these three particular families suffered from religious discrimination. Hasib was working in the United States and lost his job in December of 2000, three months after the 9/11 attacks. He has been unemployed since and living with his parents at home. His reaction:

> Do you think it is just a coincidence that I lost my job right after 9/11? I think not... it was because of my religion.... I was a 'terrorist'!

Afsana had to stop wearing *hijab* temporarily at the university out of the fear of being harassed:

> It is not fair! Where are my rights as a Canadian? Does it mean that I am less than a Canadian?

Elma supports a strong Muslim network for young adults in Canada and in the States:

> We (Muslims) have to be strong.... Growing up I always heard comments such as 'Muslims are crazy', "Muslims are stupid'. We have to fight this racism together regardless of our ethnic backgrounds. We are Muslims first, Bangladeshi or Pakistani-Canadians second.

The children are more vulnerable to open racism than their parents as they interact more with the larger society. The emphasis of religion in combination with growing up in a hostile predominantly Christian environment with Muslim peers with an Islamic support network, has tended to produce a Canadian-born generation more rigidly identified as Muslims than their parents. Shoilee Khan (2005), a daughter of Bangladeshi immigrant parents, born and raised in Calgary, writes:

> ... there is no modern Muslim! It's just us–dare I say pathetic Muslims pretending that Islam–a perfect way of life isn't actually perfect, that it doesn't fit the way we live today in the Western world. We somehow think that Islam–a religion not limited by time – is suddenly old, backward and extreme in this day and age. With this "modern" idea, we claim we have the right to "adjust" Islam to fit our lifestyle instead of adjusting our lifestyles to fit Islam.

Experiencing rejection and hostility from the larger society, this Canadian-born generation embraces a resurgence of Islamic pride coupled with the global socio-economic power of Muslim oil producing countries; a power which has had impact on both Canada and the United States. They support the rise of normative Islam which re-emphasizes visible behavioral codes and dismiss the Western cultural superiority over the East. Distinctive clothing is much more prevalent among North American Muslim women than previously (Abu-Laban, 1991: 22). Afsana wears the *hijab*, and her mother does not. As a consequence of family adaptation to mixed traditions as well as their own exposure to the ethnocentric hostility from the larger society, this generation seeks refuge in their powerful part of the ethnic identity–the Islamic identity. In the process they lose their Bengali identity, which fails to be a source of power in North America.

The ethnic identity within the Muslim community provides a subtler form of differentiation among the Muslims from Africa, South Asia and Middle East. In order to unify, the new generation of Canadian-born Muslims want to focus on the similarities between all Muslims–the religion-rather than identifying with different ethnic origins. Ethnic differences exist among Muslims in North America, but rituals and values hold them together. Asma Gull Hasan emphasizes on this issue:

> We must distinguish between what is culture and what is religion. In order to be both American and Muslims, we are going to have to let go of certain aspects of our ethnic cultures, of Islam and of our American culture. If we don't make some hard choices we'll end up being confused and in denial. I can't ignore the fact that I'm Pakistani, or that I'm Muslim, or that I am an American. Yet it is a great challenge to strike a balance among those value systems (Hasan, 2002:132).

Some of the Canadian-born Muslim youth of Bangladeshi origin see Islam as a political weapon, a strategy for physical and spiritual survival, and a way of life that can be used in their struggle for religious freedom as well as a tool to establish a powerful Muslim community in North America. Muslims in North America face the reality of living with negative media portrayals of Islam, Muslim countries and Muslim leaders (Abu-Laban, 1991: 27). Canadian-born children of Bangladeshi immigrants, along with other Muslims from this generation, have developed a very strong Islamic identity in order to create a powerful socio-political network for Muslims in North America. They are more likely to respond to the hostility expressed by the larger society by an open an organized outrage.

CONCLUSION

The Muslim community is not a monolithic group in North America; indigenous and immigrant segments of the Muslim community respond differently to some of the challenges facing Muslims in this continent. Instrumental theory of ethnicity can partially explain the current resurgence of Islamic identity among some young Canadian Muslims; however, it does not explain the loss of ethnic identity based on nationality.

Most of the studies carried out in the eighties and early nineties (e.g., Abu-Laban, 1991; Barazangi, 1991) hypothesized that Muslim youth, like youth of other immigrant parents, identify primarily with American or Canadian values and secondarily with the Islamic value system their parents communicate. However, since 9/11 some[9] of the Canadian-born children of the Bangladeshi immigrants turned out to be strict 'Muslims'. Further, they consider themselves 'Muslims' rather than 'Bangladeshi-Canadians' or just 'Canadians'. Their ethnic identity is based on their religion rather than their ethnicity. This is particularly interesting because these Canadian-born children are more religious than their parents! Since 9/11 these children (they are mostly CEGEP and university students) are becoming more politically active which is also very significant.

Some of the Canadian-born adult children of Bangladeshi immigrants in Montreal have developed a very particular identity, which is different from their parents. They have lost a significant part of their Bangladeshi heritage, and instead they were encouraged by their parents to tend to their Muslim identity. The experience of discrimination and unfairness has nudged them closer to their Muslim peers for support and affirmation. The issue seems to have gained importance in the community since the 9/11 attacks and the war in Iraq. In order to develop solidarity with fellow Muslims, and to fight existing religious stereotypes and discrimination, these young adults are eager to change their ways of life to the point that they adopt an Islamic code of ethics, consciousness, and dress code to reflect their religious affiliation. These young Canadian-born Muslim adults see their membership in the Muslim community as a superior identity to their Bangladeshi ethnic identity. For political reasons, these individuals are prone to perceiving their Islamic identity to be in conflict with their Canadian identity, and hence simply choose to be 'Muslims' rather than 'Canadian-

Muslims' or "Bangladeshi-Canadian Muslims'. Their sense of unity is evident in their common faith in *tawhid* (unity of Allah), and in their collective practice of Islamic rituals and in the expression of solidarity on issues affecting all Muslims living in Canada. An increasing sense of frustration and disillusionment has led to a growing number of Canadian-born young adults to actively commit to an Islamic identity.

NOTES

1. In Quebec, after completing ten years in high school, students attend CEGEPs for two years before entering university.
2. In many cases, parents used the exact English term 'free-sex'.
3. Like some of the other respondents, this is the term she used to identify non-Muslim outgroups.
4. Group prayer.
5. Most of them speak broken Bengali with an accent.
6. It is polite to speak Bengali with elders.
7. Learning Arabic is essential in order to be able to read The Holy Quran.
8. Syracuse University has become the first American educational institution to close on Eid al-Fitr.
9. A minority group in the community.

REFERENCES

Abu-Laban, Sharon. M. (1991), Families and Religion Among Muslim Immigrants and Their Descendants. In Earl H. Waugh, S. Abu-Laban and R. Qureshi (Eds.), Muslim Families in North America (pp. 6-31). Ontario:John Deyell Company.

——. (1975), Stereotypes of Middle East Peoples: An Analysis of Church School Curricula. In B. Abu-Laban and F. Zeadey (Eds.), Arabs in America: Myths and Realities (149-70). Wilmette, Ill: Medina University Press.

Akram, Susan. (2002), The aftermath of September 11, 2001: The targeting of Arabs and Muslims in America. Arab Studies Quarterly, Spring/ Summer: 61-118.

Barazangi, Nimat Hafez. (1991), Islamic Education in the United States and Canada: Conception and Practice of the Islamic Belief System. In Yvonne Yazbeck Haddad (Ed.), The Muslims of America (pp-157-173). New York: Oxford University Press.

Cooper, Mary H. (1993), Muslims in America, CQ Researcher, 30 April: 374.

Driedger, Leo. (1987), Ethnic Canada: Identities and Inequalities. Toronto: Copp Clark Pitman.

Fleras, A. and Elliot, J. L. (2002), Unequal Relations: An Introduction to Race and Ethnic Dynamics in Canada. Toronto: Prentice Hall.

Hargrove, Barbara. (1983), Families in the White American Protestant Experience. In William V. D'Antinio and Joan Aldous (Eds.), Families and Religions: Conflict and Change in Modern Society. Beverly Hills: Sage.

Hasan, Asma Gull. (2002), American Muslims: The New Generation. New York: Continuum.

Hashmi, Taj. (2005), Bangladesh: The Next Taliban State. Dawn, February 9.

Helly, Denise. (2004), Are Muslims discriminated against in Canada since September 11, 2001. Canadian Ethnic Studies Journal, March 2004.

Karim, Karim H. (2000), Islamic Peril: Media and Global Violence. Montreal: Black Rose Books.

Kenny, L.M. (1975), The Middle East in Canadian Social Sciences Textbooks. In Arabs In B. Abu-Laban and F. Zeadey (Eds.), America: Myths and Realities (pp.133-48). Wilmette, Ill: Medina University Press.

Khan, Shoilee. (2005), Modernizing Islam in a Modern World. Young Muslims. July 11.

——. (2002), I Told You I am Canadian. SNN Student Magazine, April 2.

Mazrui, Ali. A. (1996), Between the Crescent and the Star-Spangled Banner: American Muslims and U.S. Foreign Policy. International Affairs 72.3: 498.

Rahim, Aminur. (1990), After the Last Journey: Some Reflections on Bangladeshi community Life in Ontario. Polyphony, 12: 8-11.

Said, Edward W. (1981), Covering Islam: How the Media and the Experts Determine How We See the Rest of the World. New York: Pantheon.

Simon, Walter B. (1975), A Sociological Analysis of Multiculturalism. In Paul M. Migus (Ed.), Sounds Canadian: Languages and Cultures in Multi-ethnic Society (pp. 3-22). Toronto: Peter Martin Associates Limited.

INDEX